Attention Deficit Hyperactivity Disorder

Second Edition

Attention Deficit Hyperactivity Disorder

What can teachers do?

Second Edition

Geoff Kewley

 David Fulton Publishers

David Fulton Publishers Ltd
The Chiswick Centre, 414 Chiswick High Road, London W4 5TF

www.fultonpublishers.co.uk

David Fulton Publishers is a division of Granada Learning Limited, part of ITV plc.

First published in Great Britain in 1999 by LAC Press, Horsham
Second edition published 2005 by David Fulton Publishers

British Library Cataloguing in Publication Data
A catalogue record for this book is available from the British Library.

ISBN: 1 84312 346 0

10 9 8 7 6 5 4 3 2 1

Typeset by RefineCatch Limited, Bungay, Suffolk
Printed and bound in Great Britain by Ashford Colour Press

Contents

Preface

Attention Deficit/Hyperactivity Disorder or, more commonly, its acronym, AD/HD, is now a much used (and misused) term. There has been a great deal of myth and misinformation regarding the basic nature of AD/HD and the medications used to treat it. Notions such as 'All children can concentrate if they try hard enough', 'With adequate supervision all children can behave' and 'If there are behavioural problems it is the fault of the parenting', have been widespread.

The debate has now moved on and AD/HD is now recognised as a condition of brain dysfunction, probably involving multiple sites in the brain. It presents a wide variation of symptoms and difficulties within the classroom setting: some children are just inattentive, some are impulsive and inattentive, and in others the hyperactivity often lessens with time. Many children have other complications or conditions, the symptoms of which overlap and interlock.

The presence of AD/HD can present significant barriers to a child's learning and achievement, and it is extremely important for teachers and other professionals working with children to be aware of it, and to understand how to manage it appropriately. In schools, a proactive approach to support learning and enhance the development of social skills and self-esteem can turn a negative situation into a very positive one. Much can be achieved where teachers and support staff, medical practitioners and parents collaborate well in the management of an individual child.

This book outlines clearly the core features of AD/HD, along with the complications or coexisting conditions that frequently occur and which may impact on the classroom situation. It explains the rationale for the use of medication, emphasising that this should only be prescribed after a comprehensive assessment. There is clear advice for teachers on educational strategies for the child with AD/HD, and a 'troubleshooting' chapter considers specific situations that teachers may have difficulties dealing with. Above all it emphasises the reality of having AD/HD, the validity of the condition and the fact that untreated AD/HD represents a very considerable hidden handicap, but also that it is a very treatable condition, and that treatment greatly improves the outlook for these children.

Acknowledgements

The team at the Learning Assessment and Neurocare Centre has developed many of the concepts in this book. Particular thanks go to Pauline Latham for her never-ending supply of supportive ideas, constructive comments, tireless unofficial editing and clarity of thought regarding the various issues that are pertinent to different professionals and the families living with AD/HD; Cathy Stead for endless patience and speed in typing and retyping and juggling the intricacies of computer programs and a wide variety of sources of information into a draft text. Also to Zara Harris, occupational therapist, for guidance in handwriting issues (pp. 75–7). I would also like to thank Katherine Pate for her effective editing of the text.

I would particularly like to acknowledge the many children and their families who have, by virtue of their various difficulties and resolutions, helped me to piece together the jigsaw of AD/HD, which forms the basis of this book. The contrast between their difficulties prior to effective AD/HD management and the delightful personalities and competencies that clearly show through once effective management is given, is very gratifying and humbling.

Disclaimer

Every effort has been made to make the book as comprehensive as possible. This text is intended to educate and to act as a source of general information, relevant at the time of printing. It is not intended to be a substitute for specific professional services or consultation, nor as a means of making a self-diagnosis.

Introduction: Profiles of 'typical' children with AD/HD

Recognising AD/HD

AD/HD is still thought of as 'hyperactivity' (or hyperkinesis) in some circles. However, in recent years it has increasingly been realised that hyperactivity is but one of the three core AD/HD symptoms; the others – impulsiveness and inattentiveness – are in their own way equally important. The broader concept of AD/HD takes into account the fact that other coexisting conditions occur frequently with AD/HD and add to the child's degree of impairment, e.g.:

- excessively oppositional behaviour
- depression
- specific learning difficulties
- Asperger's Syndrome
- low self-esteem

Children with AD/HD, therefore, present a wide range of difficulties; each one is very individual. However, there are some fairly typical threads to the most common variations of AD/HD and these are illustrated in the case studies on the following pages.

| CASE STUDY | **Horace** |

Horace lives in a blur of activity and noise. In nursery school his constant running about didn't matter so much, but now that he has to sit still longer in class he is always getting into trouble for being 'disruptive'. He talks incessantly at home and in class and is always interrupting, but these interruptions are never to the point. When he has friends round, he's the one being rowdy, not that he has many friends any more. The other children say he's nasty and doesn't stick to the rules when they play games. You can't let him go to the park on his own either; he's always falling out of trees or roller-blading on the busy road.

His parents say:

- 'He's like Tigger in *Winnie the Pooh* – always bouncing. We just don't know what to do with him.'
- 'We should have guessed he'd be like this: it was like a Manchester United football match while I was carrying him.'
- 'If he'd been our first, he would have been an only child.'
- 'What wears us down most is his non-stop talking. We never get any peace.'
- 'I tell him off for something and he goes and does the same thing again within two minutes.'
- 'He becomes bored so easily.'
- 'We have been through so many babysitters.'

His teachers say:

- 'If he wasn't in my class, life would be so much easier – he causes me more stress than the rest of the class put together.'
- 'He needs supergluing to the chair to make him sit still at school.'
- 'Everybody laughs at him – the other children set him up to do naughty things, yet he seems to have no real friends.'
- 'He is always calling out in class and often has his hand up, but rarely knows the answer.'

Horace says:

- 'I wish I was invited to parties more and had more friends.'
- 'It's all Mum's fault.'

Horace has Hyperactive/Impulsive AD/HD

CASE STUDY | **Ingrid**

Ingrid lives in a dream world of her own; if you are talking to her she looks right through you or switches off halfway through, especially if she's bored by the subject. She never gets around to starting her homework, let alone finishing it. She always has an excuse or she gets distracted by something else. If you ask her to fetch things you have to repeat yourself several times, and then she comes back with only one of the things. If it were up to her, she'd always be late for school and clubs. It's not that she doesn't want to go; she gets distracted and forgets the time. One day she can concentrate, especially if she's interested; the next day she loses her pencil case, forgets to pass on notes from school and takes hours to do one page of homework.

Her parents say:

■ 'It's as if the lights are on but no-one is there.'

■ 'We repeatedly ask her the same question and get no reply.'

■ 'She could not even look into my eyes long enough to say goodnight.'

■ 'She never has any idea where she has left things.'

Her teachers say:

■ 'She needs to put her mind to it and take notice of what is happening in class.'

■ 'She knows the topic but makes silly mistakes.'

■ 'She seems to be drowsy during the day. Is she getting enough sleep?'

■ 'Please make sure Ingrid brings her sports kit to school. I have had to excuse her twice this week from games.'

■ 'She is a brilliant reader, but she can't be bothered to pick up a book because she can't concentrate.'

Ingrid says:

■ 'I know I am not concentrating but I just can't seem to help it.'

■ 'My friends tease me and say I am off with the fairies.'

■ 'The boys say, "Well, you're only a girl, what does it matter?"'

Ingrid has Predominantly Inattentive AD/HD.

CASE STUDY   Gilbert

Gilbert's parents had always known that he was very bright, and before he started school he could write his name, read books easily and understood a great deal of what was going on in the world. However, he never did well at school, and while he could put his energy into sport and other activities, where he was clearly very confident, in the classroom he was average in some subjects and below average in others. Although his parents were very concerned they were seen by the school as being over-anxious. His teachers found he could concentrate really well in some subjects, like Science and Information Technology, but in English, History and Geography, especially where he did not like the teachers, he did very badly indeed. He had difficulty in concentrating in those subjects but in other things he could over-focus.

His parents eventually transferred him to a private school with small class sizes and increased structure and support. Gilbert did very well for a while and was at the top of the year for the first two terms. However, he gradually slipped back to his old ways and was in the lower part of the year.

An educational psychology assessment showed he had an IQ of 140, putting him in the top 1 per cent of children. Thus he has tremendous ability.

His parents say:

- 'Gilbert has so much ability, yet he is often switched off and not with us and does not seem to concentrate very well.'
- 'He can concentrate on things like dinosaurs, computers and astronomy, in which he remains interested for hours and hours.'
- 'He knows so much about certain things – if only he would put it into practice, especially at school, and use his energy in the right direction.'

His teacher says:

- 'It's amazing how well he can concentrate on computers, but in English and Maths he just daydreams.'
- 'Although he is always looking out of the window, he always seems to know what we are talking about.'

Gilbert says:

- 'I don't know why I find it so hard. Some children seem to be able to get the work done in about half the time it takes me.'
- 'Having an interesting teacher makes all the difference.'
- 'I really don't think I'm very bright.'
- 'I find I get on better with adults.'

Gilbert is gifted but has AD/HD.

CASE STUDY	Melvin

Although Melvin was a whirlwind as a toddler, and his mother cut the obvious trigger factors from his diet, she wouldn't regard him as hyperactive now that he is eleven years old. In fact his AD/HD has been masked by the fact that he is so angry, defiant and easily upset, and he is getting into trouble for stealing, starting fights, hurting the cat and lighting fires. He has frequent outbursts, has virtually no self-confidence, has no friends, never gets asked to parties, doesn't get asked to play in the football teams because he has to play the rules his way, and his co-ordination is pretty poor. He now has a stutter which makes friendships harder. At school he is disruptive, easily distracted and is a long way behind. He gets some special needs help and his parents are hoping he will be given a Statement of Special Needs soon.

His parents say:

- 'I could have coped with his hyperactivity, but it is his anger, defiance and other behaviour that have caused so many problems.'
- 'He has been a handful since the moment he was born.'
- 'He even got excluded from preschool.'
- 'I am really worried that he is going to end up in jail.'
- 'He always says it isn't his fault. You can sit and watch him do something, but he still claims it is not his fault!'
- 'I don't know how I've coped without having to put him into foster care.'

His teachers say:

- 'If only he would stop and think before he answers questions in class . . .'
- 'He has been suspended three times and he will be permanently excluded next time. He is a danger to the other children in the class.'
- 'Mud sticks, and we tend to automatically blame him, though often the other children have put him up to it.'
- 'He has no sense of danger.'

Melvin says:

- 'I'm desperate to have friends, but they don't want to play with me.'
- 'I feel so embarrassed when I keep stuttering in class.'
- 'My best friend is the cat.'

Melvin's AD/HD is masked by his coexisting conditions and complications.

CASE STUDY	Toby

Toby is a nine-year-old. Just before starting school it was noticed that he did lots of shoulder shrugging and face twitching and began to sniff more and more, and to cough and spit. Before that he had always been quite active, angry and argumentative and was quite a handful. At preschool he often hit the other children and was regarded as a whirlwind, and concerns had been expressed that he might not concentrate long enough to learn.

He was also quite obsessive; he needed to line his toys up exactly in the correct position. He insisted on using a certain cup and blue plate – he had to put the milk, then the sugar on his cereal in an exact way. If he had a routine for doing something and this did not happen, he could get very upset and have a 'stress attack'.

He was being teased about his tics at school, and tried so hard to control them that when he came home they usually became a lot worse. His neck tics were so bad he even saw the physiotherapist because of neck pain. His spitting was getting worse and he kept chewing holes in his jumpers.

His parents say:

- 'Once one habit stops, another starts almost immediately.'
- 'When he walks into a room he has to check everything. If he is interrupted he has to start again.'
- 'Certainly his tics have been a real problem, but it is his impulsiveness, his obsessions and his aggression that put so much pressure on the family.'

His teacher says:

- 'On a day-to-day basis it is his concentration, easy distractibility, rudeness and hitting other children that are the main problems.'
- 'Some days he seems to be quite depressed.'

Toby says:

- 'I am so tired of being teased by the other kids. I don't understand why I'm different.'
- 'I get scared when my body makes movements I don't want it to.'
- 'I try to make my [facial] tics into something normal like a cough or a yawn so that people don't think I'm odd.'
- [To his peers:] 'Do you think I like twitching like this?'

Toby has Tourette's Syndrome.

CASE STUDY   Alexander

Alexander has always seemed different, he had difficulty maintaining eye contact with his parents when he was younger, and his speech development was slow and indistinct. He didn't enjoy being cuddled and he has always needed a set routine, especially around mealtimes, going out and going to bed. He needs the same plate and fork; he needs to have the curtains drawn and the light on and his room and his toys arranged in a very specific way.

He doesn't really seem to need friends. He doesn't relate well to people and his communication skills are poor. He is also very active and cannot sit still for very long at school and does not stay on task well. He hits other children at random.

His parents say:

- 'Some professionals say he has autism, others say he is dyspraxic, and yet others say he is hyperactive.'
- 'We just feel that if he could only concentrate and stay on task a little he might cope better with his other problems.'
- 'We always have to be careful to do things the way we know Alexander wants them done, otherwise life is unbearable.'
- 'He hates change – even Christmas and Easter – and can't cope with surprises.'

His teachers say:

- 'I can't get my fingers close enough together to measure his concentration span.'
- 'It is better when he knows what is planned ahead, and when there is a routine.'
- 'He doesn't cope well with lunchtime or playtime.'
- 'Going to school for Alexander is a real act of courage.'

Alexander says . . .
. . . very little. He doesn't seem to care what happens. However, when it comes to dinosaurs, spacemen or his favourite cartoon:

- 'I know a lot more than anybody else.'

Alexander has AD/HD and some features of Asperger's Syndrome.

CASE STUDY — Leslie

Leslie has always struggled at school because of developmental and speech and language problems. He was helped by Portage (a local service of therapists) to stimulate his development before he started school, and this was very useful. Even then it was noticed that he couldn't concentrate, that his speech development was slow and indistinct and that he tended to use the wrong words. He had been adopted, and his adoptive parents separated when he was six years old. He was said to be just like his natural father.

At school he couldn't stay on task and focus; he was in the language unit with the help of a small class size but he became more and more angry and defiant and was eventually excluded. His educational psychology assessment showed an IQ of 90 but with specific weaknesses in reading and spelling.

His parents say:

- 'We know he isn't particularly bright but we feel that if he could concentrate he could do a little better.'
- 'Although we are divorced now we noticed problems with him from one week old. We do not think our divorce is the cause of these, although it may have aggravated them.'
- 'School sees the bad work and the lack of homework, but they don't realise the hours of agony that have gone into doing it.'
- 'I was eventually asked not to bother taking him to school any more.'

His teachers say:

- 'Although he is not very bright, I think if he could concentrate he could do a lot better.'
- 'His speech is a lot better now, but he still has difficulty expressing himself.'
- 'In a one-to-one situation he improves, but in the main class he just cannot focus and he is distracted all the time.'

Leslie says:

- 'Nobody understands what I say.'

Leslie has AD/HD and Learning Difficulties.

CASE STUDY   Ted

Ted is a teenager who had been expelled for starting a fire in the classroom. He was just starting his two-year GCSE coursework but his teachers suspect he won't finish it. Over the years there have been many difficulties. He had been suspended several times, usually for starting fights and being rude to his teachers.

His parents sought many professional opinions but generally have been blamed for his poor behaviour.

Ted has become increasingly frustrated over the years, has difficulty settling down to things and getting his homework done and really doesn't have the academic basis from which to start his coursework. Concentrating, for him, is very difficult and this has been noted in most of his school reports over the years. However, it has generally been the behavioural difficulties that have gained him most attention. When he was 12 he tried to hang himself and had been admitted to the local psychiatric hospital. Ted is starting to get into trouble outside school, has been taken to the police station several times for stealing from shops and joyriding in cars. He has received several cautions and his parents are very concerned that, especially now he is no longer at school, he will end up in major trouble. He has been drinking alcohol and has experimented with cannabis. He is never at home, he can't sit still and do nothing or watch television; he has to go out with his friends.

His parents say:

- 'When he was younger I was told he wasn't hyperactive enough to get help.'
- 'We just don't feel we can trust Ted.'
- 'He has some friends but they are always the wrong types. He gets into bad company.'
- 'We know he has the ability, but he just doesn't settle down to anything.'
- 'He just has no motivation any more.'
- 'He is a real Jekyll & Hyde – loving one minute and completely upset about something the next.'
- 'Underneath it all is a lovely child trying to get out.'

His teachers say:

- 'Ted is just lazy and should try harder.'
- 'If he hits anyone else he will be expelled permanently.'
- 'I don't know how he is going to settle down to the GCSE coursework.'

Ted says:

- 'I wouldn't mind being a lawyer, because you get paid to argue.'
- 'I really just don't care any more.'
- 'I can't understand why I can do some things and not others.'
- 'School is a real drag; I just want to get out and get a job.'

Ted's AD/HD was diagnosed late as a teenager.

Arnold was 40 when, after his child Jack had been diagnosed with AD/HD, he realised that he probably also had a similar problem. When he was at school he found he could always do well if there was a teacher or subject he liked, and although he did no work and was suspended several times, he managed to get through his GCSEs reasonably well, after which he had many jobs. He later found he was exceptionally good at computers and ran a small computer business.

Arnold became bored very easily with conversations and with relationships (he had four marriages), and although he was a reasonably respectable member of society now, he had a police record when he was an adolescent. He found that he also became depressed at times and often got into trouble with people for making inappropriate remarks and for not concentrating on what they were saying. Deep down he had very low self-esteem and he found that working on computers meant that he did not have to relate to other people so much.

He had also had trouble with drinking too much and experimenting with drugs when he was younger, and had had so many speeding fines and car accidents that he had lost his licence on several occasions.

Money management and organisation were problems, so that running a small business had been fraught with difficulties. Thanks to a good accountant he had managed to cope. He was also disorganised in many other aspects of his life.

His wife says:

- 'He has such marked mood swings.'
- 'I wish he related to me the way he relates to his computers.'
- 'If you want to get something across to him it has to be in the first two sentences of a conversation.'

His mother says:

- 'Jack is just like Arnold was when he was young; he couldn't sit still, would often play truant from school, and his school reports always said he couldn't concentrate. He is the image of his father.'

His boss says:

- 'He's a nice chap but needs a lot of guidance.'
- 'If he is really interested he gets on and does it well.'
- 'He gets bored easily.'

Arnold says:

- 'Now I know about AD/HD I realise what I could have done with my life if my AD/HD had been recognised at Jack's age.'

Arnold has adult AD/HD.

What is AD/HD?

AD/HD is an internationally recognised condition of brain dysfunction. Individuals with this condition have difficulties with attention and/or hyperactivity and/or impulsiveness, which are so pervasive and persistent that they significantly interfere with everyday life. Such problems give rise to educational, behavioural and other difficulties, usually showing up in early childhood. They are more commonly diagnosed in boys than in girls, although this may partly be due to 'under-recognition' of the problems in girls.

A diagnosis of AD/HD is a clinical diagnosis – there being no blood test or scan that is diagnostic – and for this diagnosis to be made one or more of the symptoms below must be present and causing significant difficulty in everyday life, and there must be no better explanation for the symptoms apart from AD/HD.

At least 60 per cent of children with AD/HD also have other coexisting conditions or complications. The symptoms of these frequently overlap and impact on a child's ability to cope with school and home life. Such coexisting conditions include:

- excessive oppositionality
- disruptive behavioural disorders
- anxiety or depression
- specific learning difficulties
- obsessions
- developmental co-ordination difficulties
- speech and language problems.

For more about common coexisting conditions, see Chapter 2.

They frequently mask or camouflage the underlying AD/HD core symptoms, which can make accurate diagnosis, assessment and recognition of a child's problems quite difficult.

AD/HD is often familial – it appears that genetics and biology tend to create a vulnerability that can be compounded by difficulties in the child's environment. This new understanding has led to a major shift away from the previous approach of blaming parents for a child's problems towards an appreciation that many children have innate difficulties that cause problems, and that parenting such a child is often very difficult.

For more about the causes of AD/HD, see page 95.

However, much myth and misinformation about conditions such as AD/HD, and the medications that are sometimes used as part of their management, have made it very difficult for teachers and parents to gain factual information on the condition and the best way of helping an individual child.

AD/HD is an eminently treatable condition. The two strategies that have been shown to be helpful are behavioural management and medication, especially when used in combination.

For more about the management of AD/HD, see Chapter 4.

Symptom patterns

Children with AD/HD present with a wide range of symptoms and coexisting conditions but tend to fall into four broad groups:

Hyperactivity only

These children are usually extremely active. They are usually quite young, but there is also an older, often adolescent, group whose physical hyperactivity has not improved with time. (See Horace, p. 2.)

Mainly impulsive, hyperactivity diminishes with time

These children tend to have been hyperactive or overactive as pre-schoolers, but this has lessened with time. They have persistent difficulties with concentration and impulsiveness. As time goes by their self-esteem, social skills and educational ability usually worsen and they become increasingly disruptive and often anti-social. (See Ted, p. 9.)

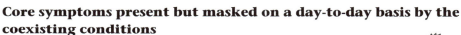

Predominantly Inattentive AD/HD (often known as ADD)

These children have never been hyperactive or impulsive, but are just unable to concentrate in some situations. They daydream, are 'spaced out' and are not sufficiently focused to take part in learning or even in life generally. This type of AD/HD is more common in girls. Because they are not disruptive they are more likely to go unrecognised, and thus untreated. Research suggests that if Predominantly Inattentive AD/HD were fully recognised, the incidence in boys and girls would probably be more equal. (See Ingrid, p. 3.)

Core symptoms present but masked on a day-to-day basis by the coexisting conditions

For example, in some children with AD/HD the associated learning difficulties, oppositionality, conduct disorder, poor social skills, low self-esteem and other difficulties can overshadow and mask the underlying core AD/HD symptoms. Of all the groups, this one is particularly under-recognised at present. (See Melvin and Gilbert, pp. 5 and 4.)

Causes

Attention Deficit/Hyperactivity Disorder frequently runs in families. A significant body of international research, using various scanning techniques, links AD/HD symptoms particularly to differences in activity in the forebrain, an area associated with concentration, time awareness and impulse control. There seems to be a malfunction in the brain neurochemical messengers that regulate these traits.

Genetic, brain-imaging and psychological research have started to converge to develop a theoretical model of AD/HD as largely a problem in response inhibition. Abnormalities of brain structure and function, generally involving the fronto-striatal pathways, have been shown by brain-scanning techniques. These studies are complemented by genetic studies showing heritability and, more recently, specific gene abnormalities, especially involving the dopamine system.

Many professionals and, to a large degree, society in general have tended to attribute children's behavioural problems to purely psychological or social problems, often complicated by poor parenting, teaching or environmental factors. However, in recent years the increase in evidence that there is a biological basis for much of children's behavioural and educational difficulties has meant a change in thinking regarding the causes of these problems.

There are also national differences in the percentage of children diagnosed with the disorder, partly because different criteria are used. Some of these national differences may reflect real differences in incidence in countries such as North America and Australia because of emigration factors. One theory is that, in past centuries, the more impulsive risk takers were more likely to emigrate or become involved in antisocial activity that would have led to their transportation. This group would probably have had a higher incidence of AD/HD, which would have been inherited by subsequent generations.

> If one child in a family has AD/HD there is:
>
> - a one in three chance of each subsequent child having AD/HD
> - a 30–50% chance that one or other parent has the condition

Core features of AD/HD

Research suggests that the basic problem in AD/HD lies in inhibiting inappropriate behaviour and controlling impulses. Its core features are inattentiveness, hyperactivity and impulsiveness. For a diagnosis of AD/HD there can be inattentiveness alone, hyperactivity and impulsiveness alone, or all three features together. They will be:

- causing difficulties for the child in two or more settings, but not necessarily all the time;
- excessive and significantly interfering with everyday life;
- inappropriate for age and developmental level;
- not due to any other reason; and
- present, significantly, for at least six months and usually have become obvious before seven years of age.

> For more detail of research into AD/HD, see Appendix 2.

> Core features:
> - inattentiveness
> - hyperactivity
> - impulsiveness

The essential features of AD/HD are outlined in the Diagnostic and Statistical Manual of the American Psychiatric Association (see Appendix 3). There are nine inattentive criteria and nine hyperactive/impulsive criteria. In either case, six of the nine criteria must be met for a diagnosis to be made. These criteria are described more fully on pages 100 and 101.

Inattentiveness

Everyone can be inattentive at times, but children who meet the inattentive AD/HD criteria usually have significant difficulties, not only academically but also in life generally, both at home and at school. Children with other conditions such as dyslexia or speech and language problems can be inattentive in an academic setting, but children with AD/HD are inattentive in many more situations and this is the cause of their difficulties. Research shows that 30 per cent of children with AD/HD have never been hyperactive and that their main problem is inattentiveness. Others may have been hyperactive or overactive when younger, but this has decreased with time, while their concentration and distractibility difficulties persist at school. The criteria for a diagnosis of inattentivity are described on pages 16–17.

'Concentration is the supreme art because no other art can be conceived without it – whilst with it anything can be achieved.'
The Inner Game of Tennis, W. Timothy Gallwey

'A notable feature in many of these cases . . . is a quite abnormal incapacity for sustained attention. Both parents and school teachers have specially noted this feature as something unusual.'
G. F. Still, 1902

Hyperactivity

'He needs supergluing to his seat.'
'He can always find an excuse to sharpen pencils or go to the toilet and just can't sit still in class.'
'He bounces off the walls.'

Diagnosis of hyperactivity requires careful evaluation of everyday behaviour in school and at home, as well as in the consulting room on the day of assessment. Only a small proportion of children diagnosed with AD/HD in clinics are actually hyperactive during the assessment.

While hyperactivity is very frequently a major problem for children with AD/HD, it is important to recognise that excessive inattentiveness and impulsiveness can be equally problematic. Sometimes parents consider that they can manage a child's hyperactivity, but it is the impulsiveness, inattentiveness and other complications that are more problematic for the child. Hyperactivity frequently becomes less obvious as the child gets older.

Impulsiveness

'The serious danger which these children constitute to both themselves and to society calls for active recognition.'
G. F. Still, 1902

Excessive impulsiveness means that the child acts, speaks or has an excessive emotional reaction without thinking. Many scientists feel that the basic defect in many children with AD/HD is their difficulty in inhibiting behaviour and the inability to stop and reflect prior to acting. Impulsiveness results in going for the most immediate goal or reward – physically, verbally or emotionally. These children have difficulty in complying with rules and tend to push boundaries and limits.

Verbal and emotional impulsiveness cause difficulty with teachers and peers. Normal discipline and other forms of behavioural management are much less likely to work for these children, because they continue to act without forethought and cannot learn from their mistakes. They do the same things over and over again, as a reflex action.

'The degree of moral control which may be perfectly normal in a very young child, may be altogether below the average for a child a few years older.'
G. F. Still, 1902

Poor social skills can be aggravated by physically inappropriate touching, clowning and doing silly things, and being socially out of tune. Many AD/HD children are 'set up' by other children at school who know that they are able to trigger impulsive behaviour and that the child will act inappropriately and be the one who gets into trouble.

Inattentive criteria

These children:

- often fail to give *close* attention to details or make careless mistakes in schoolwork or other activities.
  Things are missed out that the child clearly knows; silly mistakes occur, especially when a subject or teacher is perceived as boring. They may have jumped words or paragraphs or just scanned the words.

- often have difficulty sustaining attention in tasks or play activities.
  They have difficulty sustaining attention and are easily distracted. They may have difficulty filtering out extraneous sounds. Bright children, in particular, may focus intensely on some things that interest them but have little or no concentration for others. This does not mean that their concentration control is wilful; rather that their brains are unable to reach the concentration threshold required for apparently boring work.

- often do not seem to listen when spoken to directly.
  They seem not to listen and in class are often lost in a world of their own, missing much of what is going on. At home and in conversations they often switch off and are seen as rude and unappreciative. They frequently look straight through you and can thus appear quite antisocial in conversational style. They can sometimes be misdiagnosed as autistic because of lack of eye contact, and thus lack of communication. Parents know that they have to get their message across early in the conversation.

- often do not follow through on instructions and fail to finish schoolwork and chores (but not because of oppositionality or failure to understand).
  They fail to finish schoolwork because they get distracted and bored. They cannot be asked to fetch more than one thing at a time; they will start things and not finish them, often because they are distracted by something else.

- often have difficulty organising tasks or activities.
  Although they often know where items are beneath the piles of things in their bedrooms, children with AD/HD live in the 'here and now'. They have difficulties managing time and in thinking and planning ahead. They may forget appointments, arrive late, not have planned their day, week, month or even their next minute. Their inability to appreciate time and to think ahead is felt to be an extremely important aspect of AD/HD and one that creates many difficulties for the child.

- often avoid, dislike or are reluctant to engage in tasks that require sustained mental effort (such as schoolwork or homework).
  Actually engaging the brain in mental activities is very hard, and their chronic procrastination is extremely frustrating for parents and teachers. It can sometimes take several hours to engage the child in five or ten minutes' homework because of this difficulty. They find multiple excuses, such as going to the toilet, sharpening pencils etc. and, very often, homework time is the cause of much argument in the household. Teachers may fail to appreciate the effort that has gone into a small amount of homework.

- often lose things that are necessary for tasks or activities (e.g. toys, school assignments, pencils, books or sports equipment/kit).
  Loss of concentration, and distractibility, means that children with AD/HD tend to lose things that they need for schoolwork and other activities. They put something down and move on to the next thing, or they daydream and get distracted.

- often are easily distracted by extraneous stimuli.

Some children with AD/HD seem to have difficulty in filtering inputs – so the teacher's voice is not easily differentiated from the birds singing in the trees, the boy whispering behind or the music playing next door. However, other such children are able to concentrate better in a noisy environment. They are very easily distracted. Many children with AD/HD are also distracted by their own thoughts – especially children with high IQs who often pick up the gist of what is going on in the classroom very readily but then switch off to focus on something that is much more interesting to them. The inability to stay on task for more than a brief period of time may make the child appear disruptive in class.

This variation in the ability to concentrate, depending on the situation, is important diagnostically. Whereas children without AD/HD are able to make themselves concentrate on 'boring' things, children with AD/HD have difficulty with this; they tend to have more difficulties in listening skills than in visual concentration skills.

- often forgetful in daily activities.

Children with AD/HD have a poor short-term memory. They forget to pass on phone messages, miss outings and forget their homework. They often have enormous trouble in starting things, put things off and have great difficulty in getting organised for work or school. They tend to need to re-read things. They see the words but they do not seem to take them in. They can be drowsy in the daytime, and their work is often inconsistent with very good and bad days. They often have real problems with short-term working memory and so they tend to forget what they are just about to do, much more so than do other people.

Hyperactive criteria

These children:

- fidget.
  Many children become less hyperactive with time and by the age of 9 or 10 may be just fidgety. Fidgeting (sometimes called 'rump hyperactivity') can, nevertheless, be very annoying.

- frequently leave their seat in class.
  This is often not noticed in younger children, because the class management allows more moving around (sharpening pencils, going to the toilet etc.). However, as the child gets older he/she is not able to roam around, and this can cause difficulties and make him/her appear wilfully disruptive.

- often run about or climb excessively in situations in which it is inappropriate.
  Especially as preschoolers, hyperactive children are always running, often climbing and getting into dangerous situations without any forethought.

- have difficulty playing or engaging in leisure activities quietly.
  Many hyperactive children are more noisy than average.

- are often 'on the go' or act as if 'driven by a motor'.
  This is the classic description of hyperactive children, especially preschoolers, but it often becomes less of a problem, or is modified in different ways with time.

- often talk excessively.
  The 'verbal hyperactivity' of these children is often one of the most exasperating features for parents. They ramble on, frequently about nothing of any relevance. However, if asked to talk about something specifically, they often have difficulty with appropriate verbal expression.

Other common features

- Male–female differences:
  Hyperactive girls tend to have more difficulties with mood swings and emotional outbursts and tend to be less aggressive than hyperactive boys. However, when these aggressive and conduct problems occur, they can be extremely difficult to cope with.

- Early masking:
  The symptoms of some children with AD/HD may be masked at nursery school because of the high levels of activity allowed there, and the intense supervision. The high energy levels appropriate to their age may be difficult to distinguish from hyperactive behaviour. However, problems may still be occurring at home, where there is less structure. Many mothers say that their child was hyperactive in the womb, was very restless and never really seemed to sleep, and that this behaviour continued immediately after birth.

- Sleep patterns:
  Parents may have been told that their child is not hyperactive because they sleep well. However, by no means all hyperactive children have sleep difficulties. Many hyperactive children sleep well, often burnt out by the whirlwind activity of the day, especially if they have risen early in the morning.

- Decline in hyperactivity over time:
  Hyperactivity is most prominent in the preschool years and tends to decline with age, although it can persist into adulthood.

Impulsive criteria

The child often:

- blurts out answers before questions have been completed;
- has difficulty awaiting his or her turn; and
- interrupts or intrudes on others (e.g. butts into conversations or games).

Other common features:

- Physical impulsiveness:
  The child acts without forethought and seems to have no idea of cause and effect. For example, he/she may run on the road to chase a ball or to see a friend on the other side, without considering the danger. He/she may jump out of a window or pretend to be Superman, or climb a tree without thinking about how to get down. The child may frequently be a danger to him/herself, although parents have developed strategies to cope with this and to protect the child.

- Verbal impulsiveness:
  These children interrupt conversations (much more than normal children) and shout out in class, even though often they do not know the answer. They may say cruel and hurtful things to their friends without appreciating the damaging effect their comments may have, leading to resentment and poor relationships.

- Emotional impulsiveness:
  Children who are emotionally impulsive have marked mood swings and temper outbursts, often for little or reason. This may be difficult to differentiate from oppositional defiant behaviour (see p. 28), and frequently the two coexist. They may get upset very readily but forget about their tantrums quickly and then wonder why others are feeling upset, angry or resentful.

Consideration of IQ

Children with lower IQs generally find it more difficult to concentrate, but if their concentration difficulties are out of proportion to their learning difficulties the possibility of AD/HD should be considered. Treatment may enable them to function better and to achieve to their full ability. Sometimes children with low ability and very poor concentration appear, after treatment, to have more reasonable ability, which has been obscured by the AD/HD and complicated by specific learning difficulties.

Many children seen in AD/HD clinics are of above-average intelligence. In school their intelligence often appears to enable them to compensate for their AD/HD sufficiently to put in an average academic performance, though this may be significantly and unrecognised underachievement compared to their potential. Even if teachers identify this, these children do not usually qualify for special help as they are often considered to be simply lazy.

Such children tend to focus intensely on subjects that interest them, or when they like the teacher, but under-focus when they find something boring. They often achieve well in a test or one-to-one situation, but are easily distracted in group work or more open-ended tasks. In a supportive school they may cope well and their condition might only show up when they reach the more pressured and less structured environment of A-level courses, college or university.

Many of these children are often very aware of their failings and tend to have low self-esteem and problems with social skills and relationships. They may also suffer from anxiety or depression which may mask the underlying AD/HD, which is often the last thing to be considered in a bright adolescent who is struggling.

These children do have an enormous ability to be creative and to think laterally and, if handled correctly, they become extremely effective adults. However, the work required for each achievement is much greater than for someone without AD/HD. On the other hand, being gifted with AD/HD and having associated obsessive tendencies can make for great achievements.

'The teachers used to say that they had never seen such a bright pupil. They even gave her GCSE work when she was 12 years old, but it was so hard to keep her on task.'

'Subjects that hold his interest on a one-to-one level fail to engage his interest in a group situation.'

Quotes from Winston Churchill's school reports:

'His persistent lateness is disgraceful.'
'If he were to really exert himself he might yet be first at the end of term.'
'He loses his books and papers and various other things.'
'He is so regular in his irregularity that I sometimes think he cannot help it.'
'He has such good abilities made useless by habitual negligence.'

Growing up with AD/HD

The exact symptoms of AD/HD, their severity and the course the condition takes depend on many factors, including educational and social circumstances. Although originally seen as a condition of childhood, in the past decade it has been recognised that as a biological condition affecting brain function AD/HD is present throughout life. With time, environmental difficulties tend to compound, and by adulthood the core AD/HD symptoms are frequently buried under complications such as depression, anxiety and oppositional behaviour. One of the most prevalent myths about AD/HD is that it disappears at puberty. While hyperactivity often decreases by that age, many of the other difficulties are generally still present or worsening. Difficulties persist into adolescence for 80 per cent of children with AD/HD and into adulthood for 60 per cent.

Young children with AD/HD

Key features of AD/HD in young children

- Some young children show symptoms of AD/HD from a very early age.
- It can be difficult to differentiate between normal active preschool children and those that are hyperactive.
- Effective management can reduce stress levels for the child and the teacher.

'Even though he's only 2, his most common word is "No".'
'He's so active I just don't know how he'll be able to sit still when he starts school.'
'He's such a livewire I just can't get babysitters to look after him.'

Some children show AD/HD symptoms in the early weeks of life, even in the womb. This usually indicates extreme hyperactivity, often with a very poor sleeping pattern, or the early onset of persistent oppositionality and even Conduct Disorder (see page 28).

It may be difficult to differentiate between children with AD/HD and other normal children of the same age who are usually extremely active anyway. However, studies suggest that most children who are eventually identified as hyperactive were showing problems by 18 months.

Many such children show hyperactivity and behavioural difficulties at school. The extent to which a child's problems are due to difficult temperament or parenting problems is often very difficult to decide. A child with a difficult temperament can make even the most skilful parents feel incompetent and discouraged. Also, one or both parents may have AD/HD; resulting problems such as multiple job or relationship changes are, inappropriately, thought to be the sole cause of the child's difficulties.

While many preschoolers have problems with mood swings, socialising and high activity levels, if these problems persist and cause significant difficulties during this period an early assessment should be sought. Early identification and effective management can markedly reduce stress levels in the child, the classroom and the family.

AD/HD in adolescence

Key features of AD/HD in adolescence

- Hyperactivity often diminishes by puberty.
- Physical impulsiveness may diminish, but verbal and emotional impulsiveness may increase.
- AD/HD in adolescents is often masked by other factors, such as oppositionality, learning problems, low self-esteem, poor social skills, anxiety or depression.

Although hyperactivity has often declined by puberty, the other core AD/HD symptoms – inattentiveness and impulsivity – remain. Physical impulsiveness may have lessened by this age, but adolescents with AD/HD are likely to be much more verbally and emotionally impulsive. They will interrupt conversations, speak out of turn and lose friendships because of inappropriate remarks. They explode and have frequent tantrums, and often seem immune to rational and reasoned argument. For some with AD/HD their difficulties with rule-governed behaviour mean that they push the limits, argue a lot, have difficulties with behaviour at school, are frequently excluded and may have problems with the law.

As the years go by a child's underlying AD/HD is frequently masked by complicating factors, particularly oppositionality, learning problems, low self-esteem and poor social skills. By the time the hormonal changes of puberty occur, life is extremely difficult. Motivation has usually diminished after years of persistent failure, and is often very low by adolescence. Lack of persistence and failure to follow rules and instructions also become very prominent features at this age.

Adolescents with AD/HD show a wide variety of life patterns. At one extreme are those with Conduct Disorder, who may embark on a life of crime. Others have quite reasonable social skills, thrive on a great deal of stimulation, are the life and soul of the party and have reasonable, if superficial, relationships. Others may have underachieved academically, have low self-esteem and poor social skills, and be anxious, depressed or obsessive.

> 'He puts more pressure on the family than the other three children put together.'
> 'If only he would learn from his mistakes!'

Teaching adolescents with AD/HD

The variation in the type and intensity of problems means that no two students are likely to show the same symptoms. Teachers and other professionals involved, as well as parents, have to cope with many different manifestations of teenage AD/HD and should not expect to find a single, simple solution. These students do not necessarily respond to normal management strategies and therefore tend to be criticised and punished more, leading to hardened attitudes on both sides. Teachers need to be particularly adept at using general management strategies for a wide range of children with AD/HD and this requires resources of time and energy that are often in short supply.

In the past, adolescents who did not easily adapt to rules or the requirements of higher education could leave school at 15 and find an occupation suited to their ability. Now GCSEs involve a large number of coursework assignments, over which it is all too easy for those with AD/HD to procrastinate, and the exams require them to plan ahead and to concentrate on subjects that they may not find interesting. They are therefore a real test for both the teenager with AD/HD and their teachers.

Many AD/HD teenagers make progress only after they leave school and start on a career which is more to their liking, and where they can modify their lifestyle to maximise their strengths. Hyperactive teenagers may channel their energies into high-risk or emergency service jobs. Others successfully negotiate the world of computers and information technology. Those with a higher IQ, and who were less severely hyperactive and more emotionally stable as young children, tend to have a better outlook, as do those with better social skills, higher socio-economic status and a supportive home environment with emotionally stable parents.

Common problems for adolescents with AD/HD

- **Oppositionality**
  More common in those with hyperactive/impulsive core symptoms, this is very persistent and can greatly harm relationships.

- **Conduct Disorder**
  More common in those with hyperactivity/impulsive core symptoms. Both girls and boys who go on to develop Conduct Disorder at this stage are at high risk of early involvement with the police and social services. Girls are sometimes misdiagnosed because their behaviour is generally not viewed as seriously as that of boys.

- **Anxiety and depression**
  More common in those with predominantly inattentive AD/HD. Manic depression occurs occasionally and should be considered if there are mood swings from very high to very low.

- **Poor social skills**
  These are exacerbated by associated speech difficulties, oppositionality, mood swings or learning and language problems. Difficulties with self-esteem and social skills may be the greatest day-to-day problem for gifted teenagers with AD/HD, and one of which they are very aware. Often their high IQ has enabled them to perform adequately until now.

- **Frustration**
  Teenagers with AD/HD become very frustrated, particularly by their day-to-day difficulties in their ability to perform. Their condition is beyond their control, but is frequently misinterpreted by others as wilful. Struggles in complying with rules, whether set by adults or their own peer group, add to their frustration.

- **Demotivation**
  The daily struggle for adolescents with untreated AD/HD of attending school, having difficulty socialising and the other complications, means that sometimes the mountain they have to climb is just too high. As a result they give up, becoming demotivated and demoralised. This is frequently one of the most difficult aspects of untreated AD/HD to manage effectively.

- **Need for stimulation**
  Those who are hyperactive with AD/HD may have a low boredom threshold and flit from one high stimulation activity to another. This may be an element in cases of compulsive gambling and shopping, crime, substance abuse and teenage pregnancy.

- **Drug and alcohol abuse**
  Studies show that 30–40 per cent of adolescents with Conduct Disorder or manic depression and AD/HD are subject to drug and alcohol abuse.

- **Accidents**
  Inattentiveness, excessive impulsiveness and a lack of awareness of the consequences of their actions, sometimes aggravated by substance abuse, contribute to the higher incidence of motor vehicle accidents in adolescents.

- **Teenage pregnancy**
  Girls who have AD/HD with excessive impulsiveness and low self-esteem have a higher chance of becoming pregnant as teenagers.

- **Suicide**
  The combination of excessive impulsiveness and depression in some teenagers with AD/HD may well trigger a suicide attempt and contribute to the high incidence of teenage suicide in the UK (two deaths per day). The lack of full appreciation of the consequences of their actions and the poor or impaired recollection of past experiences, together with their shorter-term view of the future and lack of awareness of time, may all increase the possibility of suicide.

- Teenagers with AD/HD can have many entrenched difficulties after years of struggling and failure at school.
- Students with AD/HD show a wide variety of symptoms. Thus teachers need to understand the basics of AD/HD and to develop both general management strategies and specific strategies for the individual adolescent.

> 'Teachers say that if he put his mind to it he could top the year.'

AD/HD in adults

The fact that AD/HD may progress into adulthood has only recently been recognised. Between 30 and 50 per cent of children diagnosed with AD/HD have at least one parent with the condition, and other members of the extended family may also have AD/HD, although this may not have been recognised. The varied patterns of presentation of AD/HD in teenagers continue into adulthood, resulting in an even wider variation in the ways people present with, and cope with, the condition.

> 'When I used to work as a nurse they called me "Supernurse" – I like being in the thick of the action and used to ask for the most difficult and exciting jobs.'
>
> 'I couldn't count the number of jobs he has had in the past ten years.'

> - Between 70% and 80% of children with AD/HD have persistent difficulties into adulthood.
> - Between 30% and 50% of children diagnosed with AD/HD have at least one parent with the condition.

The effect of AD/HD on society as a whole goes virtually unrecognised. Many adults have lived for years undiagnosed or misdiagnosed. AD/HD contributes significantly to workplace difficulties, divorce and relationship problems, job loss, unemployment, substance abuse and compulsive gambling. It greatly increases the risk of ending up in prison, and of underachieving generally. There are also the costs of the continuing provision of relatively ineffective services. When one of the commonest conditions of brain dysfunction goes virtually unrecognised, it is hard to argue that services are operating effectively.

> **AD/HD in adults**
> - Adult AD/HD is a very real and often disabling condition.
> - It contributes to workplace and relationship difficulties, and antisocial behaviour
> - Some adults with AD/HD manage to use their hyperactivity and ability to think laterally to their advantage.

Common problems for adults with AD/HD

- **Persistent inattentiveness and impulsivity with a decrease in hyperactivity**
  Such people have usually finished school with very low self-esteem and poor social skills. They have usually underachieved academically, as well as personally, and may have become quite oppositional, if not conduct-disordered. They tend to have mood swings, may be depressed or anxious, and frustrated with the way their life is going. Their low self-esteem may have led them into the wrong relationships, and their poor social skills and boredom with work may have meant multiple jobs and/or multiple relationships.

- **Predominantly inattentive AD/HD**
  This is more common in women than men. Such women tend to leave school with low self-esteem, which persists. They are prone to anxiety and depression, and may have entered employment and studies unsuited to their actual ability. They may be more prone to pre-menstrual tension and post-natal depression. Adults with this type of AD/HD have problems with organisation of everyday tasks such as housework, organising and planning the day, organising the children and remembering where things are. They may also have great problems managing their time, meeting deadlines and dealing with financial matters.

- **Persistent hyperactivivity**
  These people, usually male and often of high IQ, use their hyperactivity to their advantage. They are very effective at running (often multiple) businesses, outshining the opposition with their high energy, not needing much sleep and always on the go. However, they may have problems keeping schedules and scheduling time at home. A low boredom threshold may cause multiple job or relationship changes. Relationships may suffer.

- **Anti-social behaviour**
  These people, usually males, have often shown oppositional defiance and Conduct Disorder at an early age and possibly associated manic depression. They are very likely to become persistent offenders, often ending up in prison. US studies suggest that 40 per cent of people convicted of homicide, rape and recurrent serious crime have untreated AD/HD.

- **Poor parenting**
  Parents with AD/HD are often labelled as 'poor parents', and any family or social problems may be, mistakenly, interpreted in that light. Accurate identification and management of the condition in parents is also a vital component of overall management of the child with AD/HD. An impulsive, disorganised or depressed adult may well be a less effective parent who would find it difficult to use the strategies necessary to manage a child with AD/HD and need enhancement of their parenting skills.

Other common patterns

- Concentration problems and absent-mindedness
- Verbal, physical and emotional impulsiveness
- Anxiety, depression and low self-esteem
- Very high or very low libido
- A tendency to think laterally and achieve goals, but not in the usual way
- Workplace difficulties
- Relationship difficulties
- Drug and alcohol abuse
- Difficulties with the law
- Car accidents and speeding fines
- Poor financial management
- Problems with family life
- Dietary and weight difficulties
- Being more prone to accidents
- Disorganisation and poor time management skills
- Problems in following through and finishing things
- Academic underachievement
- Problems in child rearing, mood swings and impulsiveness

Managing children with AD/HD

Following thorough assessment (see Chapter 3) a management plan can be devised for the individual child, using the most appropriate combination from a wide range of strategies. To be successful it will require the co-operation of all involved, including teachers, parents and the wider family, as well as other professionals.

> Some professionals and non-professionals alike may see the diagnosis of AD/HD as a soft option. However, AD/HD should not be used as an excuse – rather as an explanation. Everybody is responsible for their own behaviour, but AD/HD treatment will help the child to function to his/her potential, and function more appropriately.

Possible management options.

- Educational strategies
- Behavioural strategies
- Psychological or psychiatric strategies
- Medication
- Counselling/coaching
- Alternative therapies
- Changes to diet

Educational strategies

Educational strategies are always important, whether or not medication is also used. However, their successful implementation requires the teacher to have an understanding of the basis of AD/HD and the complications involved for the individual child. Such strategies are aimed at minimising the impact of poor concentration, impulsive and overactive difficulties on the child and the classroom, and also helping with any complications that are present. They should be individualised, with the broad principles suggested by the specialist, fine-tuned by the teacher and, where appropriate, the SENCO. It is frequently necessary for the specialist and the teacher to discuss the most appropriate strategies. Most AD/HD teaching strategies are examples of general good teaching practice.

For more on educational strategies, see Chapter 6.

Behavioural strategies

At home, behavioural interventions include house rules, daily charts, time out, points and token systems, and contracts/negotiations with adolescents. A key strategy is giving appropriate commands; in order to gain the child's attention a command should be given as a command rather than a question; it should be specific and brief, and the consequences of not following it through should be indicated.

In the classroom, similar behavioural strategies are appropriate. There need to be basic classroom rules, together with structure and organisation. Daily report cards are a particularly good example of effective management, as is a token reward system so that rewards can be earned by good behaviour or by completing academic work.

Psychological or psychiatric strategies

These can be helpful with social skills interventions, improving self-esteem and where there are specific issues around family dysfunction and other environmental problems. Focusing on improving social behavioural competencies, decreasing aggression, improving compliance and gaining closer friendships and relationships can be very helpful. However, traditional psychoanalysis can be counter-productive or even destructive, as it frequently misinterprets AD/HD symptoms. For example, the forgetfulness of AD/HD may be interpreted as being negative or aggressive in a relationship, and impulsiveness may be interpreted as wilful behaviour.

Medication

Medication and educational/behavioural strategies have a proven evidence base in the management of AD/HD. Thus, if educational, behavioural and psychological strategies in themselves do not improve the situation, and the child has significant ongoing problems, other options, including medication, should be considered.

> The medical management of AD/HD is described in more detail below.

While the core symptoms of inattentiveness, impulsiveness and hyperactivity may be helped by such strategies alone, if the child remains unfocused or excessively impulsive, there is little point in attempting complex teaching or behavioural strategies without the concomitant use of medication to provide a window of opportunity. The aim of medication should be not only to improve the AD/HD problems, but also to correct, as much as possible, the symptoms and to enable the possibility of a more fulfilling life.

In most cases an initial improvement is seen after diagnosis, although after the early treatment response there is usually a realisation that, while the problems are to some degree resolved, they will not necessarily cease. The use of medication and other strategies should be monitored, and regular clinic review is essential. Once medication has stabilised the core AD/HD symptoms, it generally has a flow-on effect to many of the other complicating factors. Reassessment after a few months of treatment can better establish what residual problems are present and how best they might be addressed.

Counselling/coaching

In some cases this can be helpful in dealing with secondary problems associated with AD/HD, such as low self-esteem and demotivation, by helping the child to recognise his islets of competence and capabilities and to think more positively.

Family counselling may be appropriate when there is a significant degree of family dysfunction that has not improved with the treatment of the child's or adult's AD/HD. Such counselling should allow for the possibility of one or both parents having unrecognised AD/HD.

Alternative therapies

Although alternative therapies are frequently trialled by parents of children with AD/HD the evidence that they are effective in managing the core symptoms is sparse at best, though they can sometimes be helpful in decreasing some of the associated factors such as hypersensitivity. Nevertheless, the misinformation that has surrounded the use of medication for AD/HD means that many people try alternative therapies initially.

Changes to diet

Evidence of the benefit of dietary modification is minimal, but some parents feel that their child's hyperactivity is helped somewhat by dietary change. For young children in particular, avoidance of some foods may reduce the child's high energy levels, but not the impulsiveness or poor concentration. Anecdotal feedback suggests that diets free of colourings, preservatives and amines are likely to be the most helpful: E numbers 100–50 and preservatives 200–97 should be avoided. However, long-term studies have not shown that dietary manipulation improves the core AD/HD symptoms.

Dietary supplements have also been trialled, either as megavitamins or various fish oil-based preparations. Although anecdotal evidence may suggest an improvement in core AD/HD symptoms, this is not backed up by scientific data. Studies of mineral and vitamin deficiencies have shown an improvement in blood levels with treatment, but no improvement in the core AD/HD symptoms.

Certainly the author's clinical experience is that very few children's AD/HD is effectively helped by these therapies, although at times they can provide a more global improvement in wellbeing and in reducing irritability.

> A study at Great Ormond Street Children's Hospital in 1993 found that some hyperactive children responded to intense dietary manipulation, but it concluded that diet is not a satisfactory method of treatment for all hyperactive children and should not be seen as a general form of management.

Medical management of AD/HD

Medication is not necessary in all cases of AD/HD. However, there is strong evidence that the use of medication, combined with other strategies at an earlier stage, when there are generally fewer complications, is a more effective approach than using other strategies alone. If medication is not considered as part of the management strategy in a person with significant untreated AD/HD the condition will usually progress with a poor prognosis.

When used in conjunction with other strategies, the correct use of medication is one of the most effective forms of therapy in AD/HD. Experienced AD/HD clinics report an improvement in symptoms in 80–95 per cent of cases. This is substantiated by reports from parents, children and schools that there are very significant continuing improvements which outweigh any side effects or other disadvantages.

> Medication improves AD/HD symptoms in 80–95% of cases.

Risks and benefits

The use of any medication for any medical condition has both risks and benefits, and the treatment of AD/HD is no exception. However, it is important that side-effects are viewed in perspective and not over-emphasised inappropriately, as has tended to be the case previously. Side-effects should be noted as either short- or long-term, and should be balanced against the likely improvement in symptoms. By considering what is likely to happen to the child or adolescent if untreated, a risk assessment of treating or not treating can be made.

For more on side-effects, see page 52.

If medication for AD/HD is suggested, there is always an initial trial, to ensure significant positive effects with minimal or no side-effects, before continuation. Medications for AD/HD have been used since the 1950s. Indeed, medications such as Benzedrine were first used for Minimal Brain Dysfunction (earlier terminology for AD/HD) in 1937.

There is no evidence that the medications used to treat children with AD/HD are addictive in the doses used. Like so many other things (Tippex™, lighter fuel etc.), such medications can be misused in inappropriate hands. However, when used to treat AD/HD they are regarded by such august bodies as the National Institute of Clinical Excellence as having a low side-effect profile.

Indeed more recent studies show that it is the condition of AD/HD itself, especially with hyperactivity and disruptive behaviour disorders, that appears to increase a vulnerability to substance abuse by a factor of six. Recent studies have shown that treating such an individual's AD/HD lowers their risk of substance abuse to a level much closer to normal.

Since the 1990s AD/HD has been one of the most written-about childhood conditions. There are several hundred well-researched studies on the use of medication for the condition, as well as thousands of general articles. There has been an explosion of research and a general increase in clinical practice in recent years. The most well-documented study is that of the National Institute of Mental Health (NIMH) multi-site treatment study published in 2001. This study looked at a group of more than 600 children with AD/HD and found that in treatment of core AD/HD symptoms there was little benefit in adding psychosocial strategies to a finely tuned medication approach. However, the addition of psychosocial strategies improved other aspects of a child's management, such as self-esteem and social skills. Behavioural strategies alone were also quite significant for these factors, whereas the use of medication in a poorly monitored setting was not particularly effective.

In addition to the NIMH study, an update on the European guidelines for the treatment of hyperkinesis has recently been published which guides practitioners in the management of children with AD/HD.

For more on the findings of this study, see page 80 in Chapter 8.

Who decides?

Parents generally seek professional help after many years of concern about their child, during which they have tried to cope and have used a wide range of strategies unsuccessfully. They have often been to many different professionals for advice, to no avail. Once AD/HD is diagnosed they usually wish to explore all the available options and receive effective help.

A stimulant medication should not be prescribed until there has been a thorough assessment and diagnosis. The possible need for medication must be discussed with the family as part of developing a treatment plan. It is for the parents and the child, if old enough, to decide on whether or not to use medication, following informed discussion with their medical adviser.

It is vital that the school is informed of any decision to treat AD/HD with medication. Any medication trial must involve the school so that they can support the child and the parents.

For more on monitoring a child's progress on medication in school, see page 53.

Aim of medication

The aim of medication for AD/HD is initially to control the core symptoms and, hopefully, to have a flow-on effect to as many of the coexisting difficulties as possible. In the educational setting it aims to make the child more available for the teaching provided.

The medications prescribed are thought to work by correcting deficiencies in the brain's chemistry on a daily basis for the duration of each dosage. Medication for AD/HD cannot be compared with giving a course of antibiotics and expecting a cure. Some individuals may require medication indefinitely, depending on the severity of the condition. Others may only require medication for a shorter period and, with the stabilisation of the situation and the more effective use of educational or behavioural strategies, coupled with an improvement in self-esteem, medication may not be needed for the long term. However, it has been shown that most children diagnosed with AD/HD will benefit from the use of medication at least through their school years. Because so many children with AD/HD have the ability to switch on and concentrate on interesting subjects, once they get through the initial school years into A-levels, university or careers they find more interesting, the need for medication can lessen or disappear altogether.

The individual is monitored regularly, the benefits and possible side-effects of the treatment evaluated and the prescription modified if necessary. Giving medication for AD/HD can be compared to giving insulin for diabetes or bronchodilators for asthma.

Most of the medications prescribed for AD/HD are types of psycho-stimulant. It may seem contradictory to use psycho-stimulants in an already hyperactive child, but they correct the abnormal function in the areas of the brain that should be helping with concentration and impulse control, either by stimulating or inhibiting. The medications used appear to allow the brain's neurotransmitter chemicals dopamine and noradrenaline to work more effectively at the synapses, or nerve endings, thereby enabling actions and thought processes to take place smoothly, without being blocked and without digression and side-tracking. This gives the child 'brakes' so that inappropriate activities do not happen so often, and concentration is improved.

Research indicates that problems in dopamine neurotransmission may be responsible for most AD/HD core symptoms, although other transmitters have been implicated. There are probably many different neurotransmitter sites and abnormalities involved, accounting for the wide range of expression and differences of response of children with AD/HD.

Specific medications used to treat AD/HD

In the UK there are three main medication groups used to treat AD/HD core symptoms; these are methylphenidate (Ritalin, Slow Release Ritalin, Equasym, modified release Equasym, Concerta XL), amphetamine preparations (Dexedrine, Adderall) and atomoxetine (Strattera). These medications are internationally recognised as being indicated for use in AD/HD when other non-medical strategies have failed.

'These medications are solid, first-line bread-and-butter type medications with a remarkably benign side-effect profile and are not considered controversial. However, AD/HD is a condition with marked functional impairment, long-term morbidity and enormous consequences for the child and the family.
(Rosenberg, Holttum and Gershon, *Textbook of Pharmacotherapy for Child & Adolescent Psychiatric Disorders*)

Medications used to treat AD/HD in the UK:

- Methylphenidate (Ritalin, Slow Release Ritalin, Equasym, modified release Equasym, Concerta XL, Metadate)

- Amphetamine preparations (Dexedrine, Adderall)

- Atomoxetine (Strattera)

Traditionally, most practitioners have tended to start children on methylphenidate preparations in the first instance. The choice of preparation depends on the child's age, educational situation and personal preferences. Increasingly, the longer-acting preparations such as Concerta, Slow Release Ritalin, modified release Equasym and Adderall are being used.

Methylphenidate (MPH) is, chemically, a piperidine, which means it is very similar to adrenalin and medications such as bronchodilator asthma puffers. Published studies show no evidence of tolerance or addiction and this confirms clinical practice. Dexedrine (dexamphetamine) is an amphetamine, as its name suggests. However, it, like MPH, shows no evidence of tolerance or addiction when used in the small doses prescribed for AD/HD.

Methylphenidate

Traditionally, methylphenidate has been the most commonly used medication. Until recently it was only available in short-acting preparations, such as Ritalin. A number of preparations have become available in more recent years, such as Concerta XL, Slow Release Ritalin and modified release Equasym, which are all based on methylphenidate but have different delivery systems. They generally last through the school day, between 6 and 12 hours, and obviate the need for a child to have a lunchtime dose of medication. This has many advantages within the school setting.

Exactly which preparation is best for an individual child needs to be carefully ascertained. Slow Release Ritalin generally lasts about twice the duration of ordinary Ritalin, i.e. 6–8 hours. Concerta, which is the ultra-long-acting methylphenidate preparation, lasts for 10–12 hours in most cases. It has a sophisticated osmotic pump delivery system where the medication is delivered slowly throughout the day. With all these preparations it is sometimes necessary to use occasional top-ups of regular MPH for homework periods, or sometimes for first thing in the morning.

Amphetamines

Dexedrine has also long been used internationally in the management of children with AD/HD. This is a short-acting preparation. There is a group of children with AD/HD who either respond better to Dexedrine than methylphenidate, or experience fewer side-effects with it. However, it is only available as a short-acting preparation. Adderall is similar, but at present it is only available on private prescription. The Dexedrine side-effect profile is similar to that of methylphenidate, but it varies from child to child. In some children Dexedrine will last slightly longer than methylphenidate.

Atomoxetine

The more recent introduction of atomoxetine (Strattera) has added a further option for medical management. Strattera is classified as a non-stimulant and is becoming increasingly popular in the management of children with AD/HD. It is long-acting and lasts through the school day, generally for 24 hours. It is particularly effective for behavioural problems at the start and end of the day. Studies have shown a reasonable response to core AD/HD symptoms. The side-effects are similar, the main ones being initial lethargy or drowsiness, nausea, headache or abdominal pain. Generally, it is well tolerated and it is not abusable.

Additional medications

The use of additional medications may be considered in children with complex AD/HD once the core AD/HD is stabilised with the use of the medications described above. There is an increasing world literature regarding the necessity and effectiveness of such combinations of medications for AD/HD. They are often critical to obtaining satisfactory management of children with multiple combinations of difficulties.

Dosage

When the dosage is correctly prescribed and fine-tuned, medication should not sedate the child: rather it should enable normal brain function. Response to medication is very individual, and in some cases, even with careful dosage and timing adjustments, may not be helpful. Some children have a very significant immediate response but, in other cases, response is slower and needs much more fine-tuning. Sometimes a second medication is necessary.

The choice of medication varies on the clinical situation. However, as far as possible, the child should be prescribed a longer-acting preparation, either initially or once control is established. In practice, this means using either Concerta XL or Slow Release Ritalin, or Strattera. It may take days or even weeks to determine the correct dosage. Once the correct dosage has been found, medication should help the core AD/HD symptoms within about 20 minutes and usually an improvement in concentration and distractibility is seen. Some of the 'flow-on' effects, such as improving self-esteem and social skills and the lessening of oppositionality, may take weeks or even months to become more apparent. Once improvement is established, appropriate behavioural and educational strategies can be tailored to the child's needs. The lowest dose of stimulant that achieves the optimum result should then be maintained.

In the UK, short-acting Ritalin is available in 10mg tablets, and Equasym in 5, 10 and 20mg tablets. Dexedrine is only available in 5mg tablets that can be cut into halves or quarters if appropriate. Short-acting tablets can be crushed and/or inserted into chocolate or banana, dissolved in warm water or given with food. Treatment can be more difficult to initiate in cases where there is severe oppositionality. Metadate, another methylphenidate preparation, comes as sprinkles which can be spread on food.

If there is insufficient response to the initial medication dosage, the dose can be slowly increased. Very young children may need to start on quarter-tablet doses of Ritalin, Equasym or Dexedrine and will need tablets every three to four hours. Adjustments must be made slowly and dosage will depend on age to some extent, but is also very individual. Very occasionally a child will respond to an extremely low dose of medication, with normal recommended doses being far too high. Changes may be made if necessary, depending on feedback from teachers and parents. Increasing the dose must be aimed at treating the core AD/HD symptoms. If the suggested maximum dose of Ritalin or Dexedrine is being used with little or no benefit, the possibility of there being unrecognised complications, or the child not actually taking the medication, should be considered.

For more on additional medications for children with complex AD/HD, see page 54.

Medication should be seen as putting a floor into the situation, treating the core AD/HD symptoms and allowing other difficulties to improve gradually.

Once the individual's optimum dose and timing is established, the dose usually stays roughly the same over the years, although with age and puberty there is sometimes an increase in dosage. Further fine-tuning or adjustment may be necessary at entry to senior school, with longer school days, more homework etc.

Deciding whether or not to medicate

It is important when deciding whether or not to undertake a trial on medication that parents understand that there has been considerable myth and misinformation in the popular and the educational press regarding the use of such medications. For teachers, a common misconception is that if a child can concentrate on interesting subjects or on computers he or she should be able to concentrate on anything else. While most children will concentrate better if they are interested, children with AD/HD are simply unable to concentrate on 'less interesting' topics. The inability to concentrate has sounded like a rather weak difficulty and something that could improve if the child tried harder. This has often been over-exaggerated in the press with the assumption that the AD/HD concept is pathologising normal childhood behaviour. In fact, nothing could be further from the truth.

The concept of AD/HD does represent quite a shift of attitude among educators. In addition, side-effects have tended to be over-exaggerated. Sometimes more side-effects occur than should have been the case because of the lack of ability to fine-tune medical management. Side-effects must always be put in context and can be minimised with good collaboration between teachers and the medical profession. The use of the longer-acting preparations has also helped to minimise side-effects.

The child's welfare is paramount, and if a child is failing at school because of AD/HD the most effective way of helping him/her should be considered, irrespective of professional boundaries.

Getting the best results from medication

> Fine-tuning adjustments of medication timing and dosage are critical to effective management.

Fine-tuning of dosage and timing is essential to successful management. With the short-acting medication it is important that dosage and timing allow continuous coverage during the day. There may be a need, for example, to give a second dose at morning break if medication is wearing off by late morning. Some children seem to be able to tell when the medication starts to work or to wear off, but others do not notice and are only aware of an improvement because of the comments of those around them.

Mornings can be a particularly difficult time of the day for many children with AD/HD, as the medication from the previous evening has worn off. Difficulties can be minimised by giving a small dose of medication on waking, followed by the main dose as the child leaves for school.

> The side-effects associated with AD/HD medication are transient, lasting for the duration of the dose.

Doses can be safely overlapped in order to avoid periods in the day when the child is unmedicated, or the rebound effect, where some children become more hyperactive as the medication wears off (see page 52).

The doctor should give parents clear, concise written instructions and limits of medication dosage to work within. It is generally appropriate for parents to make medication changes within these guidelines, following specific guidance from their medical consultant. Advice should be sought if side-effects persist or if there are problems in dosage adjustment. Most side-effects are transient and can be aggravated by too rapid an increase in dose or too high a dose. There may also be other problems related to timing or short duration of the medication.

If the expected response is not obtained, the dosage may be too low or the timing may be wrong, or it may be that medication is not suitable for the child and alternatives will need to be considered. It may be that, in fact, the core AD/HD symptoms – concentration, impulsiveness and hyperactivity – have been improved, but that the residual difficulties lie with coexisting problems, such as oppositionality or obsessions. If a child refuses to swallow tablets because of oppositionality, this is then sometimes treated first so that the child or adolescent is more amenable to the overall concept of medical treatment. The use of longer-acting preparations has tended to minimise many of the difficulties mentioned above. However, the longer-acting preparations may still need to be combined with some shorter-acting medication to obtain the optimal result. The dose of such medications varies widely. Children with predominantly inattentive AD/HD tend to need lower doses than those with more hyperactive types.

Giving medication at school

Most children with AD/HD need to take some of their medication at school, though with the use of longer-acting medications this is now less common. The attitude of the staff and whether or not they are supportive of the use of medication, with other strategies, can be extremely important. The child needs to be able to take medication without being teased, bullied or having attention drawn to it. Rather than saying 'Johnny, it's time for your tablet', discreetly drawing the child aside or having a set routine that does not draw too much attention to him/her is far preferable. Some children find an alarm-watch – possibly one that vibrates and that can be set for a number of times – or even a bleeper useful. However, because AD/HD children tend to lose things, many children also lose their watches or forget the alarm has gone off.

The school should set up a system of safe storage so that the medications cannot be diverted to other children or staff. There should also be a system for recording the number of tablets and doses used for each child, in line with the school's health and safety policy.

Side-effects of medication for AD/HD

The medications used to treat AD/HD may have possible side-effects, as with any medication for any condition. These are rare and mainly short-term, occurring significantly in 10–20 per cent of children.

If mild side-effects occur, medication is usually continued as the problems will generally resolve themselves. If side-effects are more significant the physician may recommend reducing or stopping the medication. Teachers should inform parents of any side-effects that they observe, particularly if the child appears subdued mid-morning or if there is any rebound or wearing off effect in the late morning.

The most common side-effects are described on page 52.

Stimulant medications for AD/HD are controlled medications. The information supplied with the tablets should be read carefully. Medication must be kept in a safe place and the amount of medication must be carefully controlled.

There is no evidence that the medication is addictive at the dosage used to treat AD/HD. Once a dose has worn off, children revert to their previous difficult behaviour or poor concentration, in the same way as an asthmatic starts wheezing once the bronchodilator has worn off. Rather than craving their medication, children often forget to take their next dose, especially those who have AD/HD-associated short-term memory problems.

Short-term side-effects

Short-term side-effects may occur just for the duration of the medication or as it wears off. In practice it is the short-term side-effects that are sometimes of concern. In addition to the side-effects listed below, itchy skin, rashes, a feeling of depression, mood change or nausea can occasionally occur.

- Appetite suppression
  This is probably the most frequent side-effect. It usually diminishes over the first few weeks of medication, but it can persist, though it is rarely severe enough to warrant cessation of medication. There is sometimes some weight loss over the first few months, but this usually adjusts later on. Eating frequent snacks, or eating late in the day or first thing in the morning when medication has worn off, can sometimes help, as can adjusting the timing and dosage of medication. There may have been pre-existing poor appetite, and sometimes the appetite actually improves on medication because the child is able to sit still long enough to have a meal.

- Abdominal pain/headaches
  These occasionally occur in the first few days of medication, but rarely persist. Often any headaches and abdominal pain that have been secondary to the stress of untreated AD/HD improve once treatment is started.

- Loss of 'sparkle'
  Transient change in personality can occasionally occur. Some children become irritable, weepy and quite angry or agitated, more commonly with Dexedrine. This may occur either while the medication is working or as it wears off. It can be minimised by making slow dosage adjustments, and usually improves with time or with a slight reduction in dosage. If these side-effects persist the consultant may recommend stopping the medication. Occasionally, medication may cause some particularly bright children to over-focus, particularly if the dosage is a little too high.

- Sleep difficulties
  Too high a dosage of medication too late in the day can make it difficult to settle the child for sleep. In some children even a very small dosage at midday will affect sleep, while others can take a large dose with the evening meal and still sleep well. Sleep difficulties are very much an individual problem and modification of dosage may be necessary. Occasionally, Ritalin can actually improve pre-existing sleep problems.

- Rebound effect
  Some children, especially those who are hyperactive, become even worse as the medication wears off. If significant rebound occurs it is important to ensure the doses are overlapping and this may mean a change of timing.

- Tics
  Involuntary movements or vocal tics occasionally occur with AD/HD and, if severe, may be related to Tourette's Syndrome. Although it is often thought that Ritalin aggravates them, experience shows that it sometimes improves them, and they are not necessarily a contra-indication to the use of Ritalin. Sometimes a second medication is necessary to control them. Almost always, if tics have been exacerbated by medication, they ease once the stimulant is ceased, but very occasionally they can be persistent. It is unusual for tics to be aggravated if the child does not also have obsessive tendencies (see also p. 30).

Long-term side-effects

- Possible growth suppression
  Early studies suggested that height suppression could occur on medical treatment for AD/HD, but more recent studies show that this is not the case. There is some evidence that children with AD/HD may enter puberty later, and thus their growth progress may slow down for a time. It would appear that in most cases final height is not affected, although re-analysis of recent data suggests that in some children there may be a very slight adjustment to final height.

- There is no evidence of long-term addiction, blood disorders, liver or kidney malfunctions, or other long-term difficulties with the use of the medications prescribed for AD/HD.

What to expect from medical management

Medication, in conjunction with other strategies, can produce marked change. For the first few months there is usually a very rapid improvement in the core symptoms and often in some of the other features. Generally, a chronic, intransigent situation is significantly improved so that a window of opportunity can be created for the more effective use of educational, behavioural and other strategies.

The relief that parents and teachers often feel initially when they realise that something can be done is usually replaced by the realisation, after a few months, that the problem will be ongoing, and even with treatment it may possibly be long-term. A miraculous transformation should not be expected, as there are often many difficulties to improve, which in many cases can take a long time. Ongoing monitoring and co-operation between school, parents and physician is essential.

Successful medical management should lead to:

> Medication should be seen as an essential adjunct to effective teaching of a child with AD/HD.

- Improved concentration, impulsiveness and distractibility
  The purpose of medication is to improve these core symptoms of AD/HD. Oppositionality, aggression and hyperactivity may also show improvement once the core AD/HD symptoms are managed effectively. Short-term memory usually improves, as does the ability to learn and perform at school. More slowly, there is usually an improvement in self-esteem and socialising ability, in relationships, in learning ability and in mood swings. Being off-task, not listening, impulsiveness and overactivity are decreased.

> 'My brain doesn't hurt any more.'
> 'His progress is vertical!'
> 'He can see himself as somebody now, not just the class clown.'

- Improvement in concentration and behaviour in the classroom
  If there are associated specific learning difficulties, progress may be slower. It is often very difficult to assess the severity of associated specific learning difficulties until the AD/HD is treated.

- Verbal, emotional and physical impulsiveness frequently improve
  These symptoms may be difficult to disentangle from symptoms of Oppositional Defiant Disorder, which may also be improved once the core AD/HD features are managed effectively. There is generally an improvement in verbal expression and speech clarity. More complicated language difficulties are slower to improve, but may gradually improve with time, once the child is more focused and more socially aware. Medication

'There has been a considerable metamorphosis of Adam this term. He has displayed interest and enthusiasm towards the subject. Some of his contributions during discussions have exposed a hitherto unrecognised knowledge and intuitive understanding of the subject. I can safely say that it is one of the most pleasing experiences of my professional career.'

'He is now able to go on school trips.'
'Whole demeanour is different.'
'I was choked when he got his first birthday party invitation. He's never had one before.'

Approximately 90% of children with AD/HD will show a very significant improvement. About 40% of these will have ongoing difficulties because of other coexisting conditions.

allows the situation to stabilise and then enables the residual difficulties to be helped in a more effective way.

- Improvements are maintained
  Once AD/HD is treated appropriately the improvements are generally maintained, provided a combination of strategies is used – including medication – and the situation is regularly assessed and the approach modified as needed.

- The use of medication may be long-term
  This will depend on the severity of the medical condition, the age at diagnosis, the number of complications and other factors. Once the core AD/HD is managed effectively, other problems can often be dealt with more easily. Children on medication should be regularly monitored and reviewed to assess whether or not there is continued improvement and whether the benefits of medication outweigh any other difficulties.

If there is no improvement

If the child does not respond to one medication then an alternative stimulant should be used. If the core AD/HD symptoms are managed effectively, but there is continued depression, obsessions, oppositionality or tics, then a second medication may be necessary.

Occasionally, a child who has been well controlled on a certain dose of a medication seems to develop a tolerance, or a less-effective response to medication. In this situation, changing to the other stimulant, or stopping the medication for a few weeks and then restarting, is the most effective form of management.

Medical management in specific situations

- Teenagers
  As AD/HD is a progressive condition, many teenagers are excessively oppositional and sometimes conduct-disordered, which may make it impossible to initiate medical management because of lack of compliance and excessive oppositionality. If the oppositionality can be modified, psycho-stimulants can then be introduced to improve concentration. Unfortunately, most teenagers resist parental interference at this stage and it is very difficult to remind them to take their medication. Diagnosing and then treating an adolescent with significant AD/HD for the first time in teenage years is like trying to stop a car going at 100 mph rather than at 30 mph – it takes a lot longer. There are usually a number of difficulties on the way, but after 12 to 18 months persistent improvement can be seen.

- Adults
  By adulthood, life's difficulties and coexisting and complicating conditions make management more difficult. It is never too late to treat if the severity of

the AD/HD warrants it. Overall, adults respond to medication in a similar way to children.

- Children under 6
The use of stimulants in such children has caused considerable debate and discussion. Methylphenidate is licensed for children who are six years of age and above. There is, however, a wide body of international opinion that attests to the safety and effectiveness of medication when used in children under six where indicated. The Royal College of Paediatrics and Child Health guidelines for the use of unlicensed medications are helpful in this regard.

A large, multi-site study looking at these issues is currently being undertaken in the US. Overall there are seven well-controlled studies assessing the treatment of children in this age group.

Experienced practitioners involved in the care of AD/HD children acknowledge that there is a group who need treatment at a younger age and who, in fact, often do much better if this is the case. Some studies show that children who present with the early onset of AD/HD may be a more virulent group and that they may more frequently have other coexisiting conditions, such as the early onset of Oppositional Defiant Disorder and/or learning or language difficulties, in addition to their AD/HD. Early treatment enables them to access the curriculum more easily, develop appropriate social skills and improve their learning or language difficulties.

Children with Predominantly Inattentive AD/HD

Such children may only need to be treated with medication during the school hours, for example usually with only two doses per day of short-acting medication or a small dose of a long-acting preparation, provided they cope with homework, there are no significant behavioural problems and self-esteem is reasonable. They generally respond very well, and often to very low doses of medication, unless complicated by significant anxiety or depression.

AD/HD and epilepsy

For children with epilepsy, it is often crucial to also treat their AD/HD. An abnormal EEG or epilepsy is not now generally regarded as a contra-indication of the use of stimulants in the treatment of AD/HD. Evidence that stimulants alter the seizure threshold is tenuous.

AD/HD and Asperger's Syndrome

It is less likely that such children can be treated successfully, although when it can be achieved it can make a great functional difference to the child. When the obsessions and the core AD/HD symptoms are treated successfully, this can help the child cope more effectively with the other difficulties. However, more frequent side-effects or complete lack of response are common in this group. Often a low dose of medication, combined with low-dose Fluoxetine Syrup or Clomipramine to help with the obsessions and rituals, can be very helpful.

AD/HD with severe Oppositional Defiant Disorder and/or Conduct Disorder, especially of early onset (Disruptive Behavioural Disorder)

If a child has ongoing oppositionality, impulsiveness and/or Conduct Disorder despite the core symptoms being effectively managed by methylphenidate or dexamphetamine, he/she might benefit from Clonidine, which often has the effect of decreasing the intensity and frequency of such difficulties. Originally used in high doses as a medication for high blood pressure, Clonidine is effective in low doses in 60–70 per cent of children with persistent oppositionality. Other medications that may be effective include Sodium Valproate, Carbamazepine, Risperidone.

AD/HD with associated anxiety, depression or obsessions

If anxiety, depression or obsessions persist once the core AD/HD symptoms have been treated, this may warrant the introduction of a second medication, such as Fluoxetine. In one study, 30 out of 32 children with persistent anxiety and depression after the treatment of their AD/HD received a great deal of benefit with the addition of very low dose Fluoxetine.

AD/HD with coexisting manic depression (bipolar disorder)

The stimulants prescribed for AD/HD may aggravate the manic depression. Anti-convulsants such as Carbamazepine or Sodium Valproate may be helpful as may atypical antipsychotic medications such as Risperidone.

AD/HD with tics and/or Tourette's Syndrome

The AD/HD symptoms are usually much more of a handicap to the child than are the tics. Studies show that with the use of stimulants, 15 per cent of tics will get worse, 15 per cent will get better and in the remaining 70 per cent there is no change. Clonidine is frequently effective in the management of tics. Other medications that can be used include Pimozide and Sulpiride. Tics should not be treated unless they are significantly interfering with the child's function. Often the tics will wax and wane as part of the condition and may be exacerbated by the amount of stress in the child's life.

AD/HD with substance abuse and Conduct Disorder

Although traditionally associated with one another, AD/HD and Conduct Disorder have previously only been treated after the substance abuse disorder has been managed appropriately. Now, however, there is increasing clinical experience in treating all conditions at the same time, using family and individual therapy (drug action teams) and support as well as psycho-pharmacological intervention, where appropriate. Treating the AD/HD and Conduct Disorder often allows the adolescent or adult to benefit more effectively from their substance abuse management and have no need for substances.

Professionals and services for AD/HD

Because AD/HD is such a common condition, with such a wide range of presentations, it impacts on many different professions and service providers. It is therefore essential that all professionals understand the true facts and reality of AD/HD in order to help and manage people with AD/HD under their care most effectively and to offer more effective services.

Of course, teachers have a special responsibility in the management of children with AD/HD. Up to 5 per cent of schoolchildren have the condition, making it one of the most common conditions that teachers will encounter. An awareness of the condition, a non-judgemental approach to its management and the ability to work in a seamless way with other professionals are essential. This particularly applies to special educational needs co-ordinators (SENCOs) who also need an understanding of the links between AD/HD, dyslexia and developmental co-ordination difficulties.

> In a school of 1,000 pupils, approximately ten will have severe AD/HD and at least a further 20 will have less severe variants of AD/HD.

A number of studies have shown that children in special schools, particularly schools for children with emotional and behavioural difficulties and pupil referral units, have a higher likelihood of having AD/HD. Therefore, teachers in these schools need to be particularly aware of the condition, its complexity and how it may be accompanied or even masked by coexisting conditions. There is also a high incidence of AD/HD in children who have been excluded from mainstream schools.

Educational psychologists frequently assess children with educational and/or behavioural difficulties. Again, a non-judgemental, well-informed approach to the possibility of a child having AD/HD is essential. The British Psychological Guidelines on AD/HD, published in 2000, are an important basis.

> For more on such studies, see the publications listed under 'Learning difficulties' in Appendix 1. For more on coexisting conditions, see Chapter 2.

Among medical practitioners, **GPs** have a key role, not only in initial referral for assessment, but also in continuing prescription of medication, if used, and in providing general support to the family.

A comprehensive assessment to determine whether or not a child has AD/HD should be carried out by either a **child psychiatrist** or **community paediatrician**. Both professions have much to add to the diagnosis and management of children with AD/HD, but which one is employed depends very much on the availability of local services. Since they are involved with children from birth, **health visitors** are in an excellent position to identify those who have extreme hyperactivity, early oppositionality and severe sleep difficulties. Their liaison with the general practitioner can be very helpful. **School nurses** are also critical in identifying and helping to manage children with AD/HD.

Many other therapists may come into contact with children with AD/HD. For example, as about one-third of children with AD/HD have, or have had, a speech and language problem, **speech therapists** are frequently involved. Sometimes it is necessary not only to provide speech and language assistance but also to treat the child's AD/HD. **Occupational therapists** have a similar role. In diagnosing a child with developmental co-ordination disorder or dyspraxia, they must also consider that a child who is also inattentive or hyperactive may have coexisting AD/HD.

> Munchausen's by Proxy may be erroneously diagnosed in parents of children with severe, unrecognised AD/HD.

Children with AD/HD, especially where there is the early onset of associated Conduct Disorder, are frequently referred to **social services departments**. AD/HD is common in adopted children because of genetic factors. It is also common in children with challenging behaviours. Young parents with AD/HD, especially if they also have Conduct Disorder, have higher rates of child abuse and domestic violence.

The group of people with AD/HD and associated Conduct Disorder have a much higher chance of being involved with the **criminal justice system**; thus an awareness of AD/HD is important for all those involved with the youth justice service, with magistrates, with lawyers and with the judiciary. AD/HD may compromise a person's ability to testify and give evidence. Studies show that treating AD/HD, as well as including rehabilitation programmes, greatly reduces the risks of reoffending. Involving AD/HD and dyslexic strategies in education in prison programmes is also important.

Summary

There are some children with AD/HD whose difficulties can take a while to improve, or who are a particular challenge to treat, but there is no doubt that most children who would have ended up in significant difficulties are greatly helped. Treatment with medication greatly enhances the quality of the child's relationships at home and at school, in time.

The length of time a child will need to be on medication varies. Experience seems to show that children benefit greatly if they are treated before complications arise, but there are no firm data on this. One of the myths of AD/HD is that it disappears by puberty. In reality, by teenage years it is often much worse and is compounded and masked by other difficulties. Hyperactivity has often diminished, but this does not mean there are no other problems. In fact, it is often necessary to treat teenagers and also adults, as a significant proportion of people are affected with the condition into adulthood.

Some children outgrow the need for medication during school years and many more discontinue medication when they leave school. Although many of their AD/HD symptoms may continue, provided they can get through school with protected self-esteem and reasonable academic and behavioural achievements, in later life they may be able to focus, or indeed over-focus, on things they are really interested in, without necessarily needing to continue medication.

Case studies

The case studies here illustrate a range of problems seen with children with AD/HD. They are included to illustrate the descriptions of AD/HD given in the earlier chapters of this book, and in particular the management strategies outlined in Chapter 4 and the educational strategies outlined in Chapter 6. Because of the wide range of presentations of children with AD/HD, the following case studies may be helpful for teachers in the indentification and management of a child with AD/HD.

Case studies – AD/HD and various symptom patterns

- Glen – moderately severe AD/HD, see page 58
- Leighton – combined AD/HD with early-onset ODD and specific learning difficulties, see page 59
- Chris – hyperactivity, see page 60
- James – gifted with AD/HD, see page 61

Case studies – AD/HD and other conditions requiring further medication

- Alan – combined AD/HD plus early-onset ODD and Conduct Disorder, see page 62
- Mitchell – late diagnosed combined AD/HD, ODD, Conduct Disorder, learning difficulties and substance abuse, see page 63
- Sonia – combined AD/HD, Conduct Disorder, anxiety, pregnancy, see page 64

Moderately severe AD/HD

History

Glen's mother had worked for many years in a school for children with emotional and behavioural difficulties. When Glen was 12 years old she realised that AD/HD was a common, underlying factor in many such children and she noted that, although Glen was in mainstream school, he was struggling. His concentration was very poor and his school reports repeatedly commented on his obvious ability, but his inability to put his mind to things and take notice of what he was doing. He had never been able to concentrate long enough to read a book and she felt that if he could concentrate he would learn a lot better. He was very disorganised. She said it was a month of hard work trying to tidy up his bedroom, and he had very little routine. He didn't think ahead and he lived for the moment; he often couldn't participate in sports day because he forgot his PE kit and was always losing things. Almost every week she had to buy a new set of pencils and he never had any idea of where he had left things. He had very few friends, was never asked out or invited to parties and his self-esteem was low. With the onset of puberty he was starting to become more and more oppositional. A wide range of educational and behavioural strategies had previously been tried, but without benefit.

Assessment

Glen was of average intelligence, with combined AD/HD, and 1–2 years behind his reading, spelling and maths attainments. There were no other associated specific learning difficulties, some features of mild Oppositional Defiant Disorder, low self-esteem, occasional mild motor tics and some mild obsessional features.

Management

A trial of methylphenidate and associated behavioural and educational strategies resulted in a very dramatic initial improvement in his core AD/HD symptoms and a subsequent improvement in all his other problems over the ensuing months. He started to develop more lasting friendships, to be asked out more, and his self-esteem improved. In class he was able to concentrate much better, to be better organised and less impulsive, and to achieve to his age-appropriate ability. On medication, there were some initial problems with sleeping which gradually improved, and also his tics disappeared.

In the classroom he needed basic educational support strategies with structure – seating him towards the front of the class – and clear rules and organisation. He needed help in getting his homework to and from school and was also helped with the use of a daily report card. He did need special needs support to help him catch up with his delay with reading, maths and spelling, but once he was able to catch up, with the use of medication, this made a great deal of difference to his academic achievement.

Leighton

Combined AD/HD with early-onset ODD and specific learning difficulties

History

Leighton, aged 9, had for two years been at a residential school for children with emotional and be-havioural problems (EBD), following his exclusion from mainstream school. He had been extremely active from birth, and this continued at preschool. At nursery school he became increasingly angry, defiant and oppositional, and was excluded. His mother commented that as a five-year-old he was virtually running their family life. When he started at mainstream school, his disruption, class clown-ing and poor concentration continued. He was eventually excluded, following a string of severe emotional outbursts and bullying of other children.

His parents had previously sought professional advice and the behaviour was blamed on his parents' divorce when Leighton was aged 2. The parents disputed this as they felt that his mother's subsequent remarriage had led to a continuing very stable relationship, although Leighton had put a great deal of pressure on this. Leighton's mother felt that he was very much like his natural father who had struggled at school and left early, and eventually entered jail.

Assessment

Leighton had very significant functional difficulties with virtually all of the main AD/HD criteria, both at home and even at the EBD school, despite the small class size and a great deal of structure. In addition, he had a number of other complicating difficulties including Oppositional Defiant Disorder of early onset, associated specific learning difficulties, poor handwriting and low self-esteem.

Management

1. Because of the severe, complicated and persistent history, Leighton was started on methylphenidate (Ritalin) to treat his core AD/HD symptoms. Fine-tuning of dosage and timing was necessary to avoid rebound effects. This resulted in an almost immediate, dramatic improvement in the core symptoms, such that he was able to concentrate. He reacted much less impulsively and became less hyperactive.

2. Over the next few months there was a slower, but very significant, improvement in almost all of his other problems. His oppositional symptoms became much more manageable, his handwriting improved and his self-esteem also improved, though more slowly. He had ongoing specific learning difficulties, but once he was able to concentrate he was able to benefit from the intensive educational support. He became less frustrated and angry.

3. After a further 12 months, he was slowly integrated into mainstream school. He still required the basic educational supportive strategies and needed an ongoing behavioural modification approach with a school–home diary and a daily report card. There was ongoing communication and monitoring with the school, via the school liaison officer, and significant continuous educational support via his Statement of Special Needs.

4. Supportive individual and group counselling helped Leighton cope with his AD/HD and with his previous difficulties.

AD/HD

History

Chris was a nine-year-old boy who had AD/HD with no other significant complications. He met all of the AD/HD criteria and had done so even as a preschooler. His mother had tried a number of dietary manipulations which had reduced his hyperactivity a little, and it had lessened somewhat with time; but he was still very active and was especially verbally impulsive, inattentive and highly distractible. His teachers commented that in the class 'as soon as his hand went up his mouth opened'. Although he was underachieving a little in class he was not receiving extra support. His self-esteem and social skills were causing some moderate difficulties, but there were no other complicating factors apart from poor handwriting. He was of slightly above average intelligence and achieving to just below his chronological age level.

Management

1. Educational strategies were implemented. He sat at the front of the class, the teacher cued him in, gave him brief instructions and tried hard to nurture his self-esteem. He was also supported during the unstructured playtimes, and this helped a little with his social skills, although there were still problems.

2. After a term of observation, as his problems persisted, a trial of medication (methylphenidate) showed a dramatic improvement in all of his core AD/HD symptoms, especially his concentration and impulse control. Chris was then able to achieve much more readily, educationally, and although the educational strategies were still necessary, they were able to be implemented less intensively. His self-esteem and social skills subsequently improved and he did well in the end-of-year examinations.

James

Gifted with AD/HD

History

James had been extremely active in the womb and his parents knew that he was different from a very early age. He had never been a 'real' baby, according to the parenting books, and was always trying to look around or strain his neck towards something. He wasn't particularly cuddly.

He progressed very quickly and did not walk but ran. At age 2 he developed frequent tantrums, head-banging and cried a great deal. Cutting out food colourings calmed him a little, although he was always 'on the go'. Even now, food colourings aggravate his behavioural difficulties.

He started at nursery at 2. There were lots of problems; he was always running around, and the nursery staff had difficulty in controlling him. He was bright and understood things very quickly yet displayed appalling behaviour. When he was 3, his verbal comprehension was age 5 level, and later educational assessment showed a general intelligence ability of about 130.

Starting school, aged 4 years 8 months, brought problems from the first day. He did not settle, he was disruptive, he called out and he seemed to move from one task to another without accomplishing any of them successfully. The teacher noticed his poor concentration and motivation, which contrasted with his very marked academic ability. He had very few friends, was constantly demanding attention, was unwilling to listen, was aggressive to teachers and other students, and was non-conformist. He found sitting still very difficult and was always touching things. However, his teachers noted that there was a loving, affectionate side to him and that he was a lovely character. The ongoing problems meant that he moved school at age $5\frac{1}{2}$, but the problems resurfaced very quickly. The school thought it was all due to bad behaviour and poor parenting. His educational testings at $5\frac{1}{2}$ were at nine-year-old level. His teacher noted that he had a remarkable ability at explaining concepts and in reading and mathematics, and on a one-to-one basis he showed sound and deep levels of understanding. However, in group activities he would readily become impatient and disruptive, had difficulty in focusing and staying on task and required constant supervision. At times, his behaviour was bizarre and even frightening.

Assessment

His parents became increasingly concerned that something else was wrong and that he would never fulfil his potential. They became aware of AD/HD and an educational psychology assessment was done. This showed an IQ score of 148, and thus indicated enormous ability. There was no sign of dyslexia, but his short concentration span and impulsivity were noted, as were his excellent vocabulary, number skills, sentence construction and comprehension.

Management

After thorough assessment and discussion, a diagnosis of AD/HD was made and a trial of medication (methylphenidate) was commenced. The response was impressive. His parents and school noticed a transformation and that he was a different child who now wanted to go to school. There was an immediate improvement in all the areas that had been concerning them, and the school said it was like a switch being turned on. There was such a difference in his work that he was able to achieve according to his high ability. His behaviour improved and he was no longer disruptive. Slowly, his self-esteem improved. His grandparents even offered to babysit for him for the first time!

The ongoing educational strategies involved some minor need for educational structure and support in the classroom, and, additionally, an awareness by the school that he was gifted and needed an accelerated programme to maintain his interest.

There were some ongoing social issues, partly because of his giftedness and partly because of his fluctuating self-esteem. These slowly improved with time, but he tended to need structure and support, especially during playtime. The school worked hard on nurturing his self-esteem and providing a supportive schooling environment that made a great deal of difference to him.

Over the next few years he continued to make excellent progress, both academically and socially. He still could have difficulties without structure or support, and at times socially, but the combination of medication, an understanding of AD/HD and the correct supportive schooling environment made a great difference to James.

Alan

AD/HD with early-onset Oppositional Defiant Disorder and Conduct Disorder

History

Alan, age 6, came for assessment with his mother and his social worker. He had been extremely active, even *in utero* and certainly from birth. He had been aggressive, oppositional and excessively impulsive from a very early age. The family were very stressed because of severe financial pressure, and the parents were at loggerheads. He was the second eldest of four children, all under 8. Prior to starting school a number of agencies and professionals had seen him. He had been placed on the 'at risk' register because of being hit by his father in a fit of temper after another night of his not sleeping and being persistently disobedient. Alan was struggling at school. His speech development was slow and unclear and he had a stammer.

Assessment

In addition to being severely hyperactive, Alan's teachers also noted that he had a very poor concentration span and was persistently verbally and physically impulsive. The assessment confirmed that he was severely hyperactive, had very poor concentration and was very impulsive. He had the worrying combination of early-onset oppositionality and Conduct Disorder, together with severe learning and language problems. He was placing an enormous amount of stress on an already pressurised family. There was a combination of AD/HD and early-onset Oppositional Defiant Disorder, together with learning problems and environmental issues.

Management

1. An initial trial of methylphenidate made him much more aggressive.
2. His prescription was therefore changed to dexamphetamine 5mg tablets, and by slowly adjusting the dosage and timing there was an improvement in his concentration and a marked reduction in his impulsivity and hyperactivity. His initial appetite suppression improved.
3. However, his oppositionality persisted, as did his verbal impulsiveness and sleep difficulties. The addition of clonidine in the morning and evening slowly made him less oppositional and his outbursts less frequent. He also slept better.
4. Liaison with and support from the school enabled him to continue in mainstream education with a Statement of Special Educational Needs. Alan needed a great deal of structure and avoidance of distraction, and his school was very supportive. At school, he needed two doses of dexamphetamine during the school day because the medication only lasted two-and-a-half hours and he became more oppositional during the rebound period.
5. Supportive and marital counselling were given through the local guidance services and the parents were also given help with parenting strategies.
6. The family were eventually rehoused two years later.

Parents commented that just having Alan sleeping put significantly less pressure on the family; they were less tired and were able to cope better with some of the difficulties. This, together with a mellowing of his oppositionality and aggressive behaviour, greatly improved the family functioning. With his increased concentration at school he benefited much more from the support offered to him and achieved much more in class.

Mitchell

Late-diagnosed combined AD/HD, ODD, Conduct Disorder, learning difficulties and substance abuse

History

At 15 years of age Mitchell had been permanently expelled from school for fighting with other children. He had even been expelled from preschool and playgroup and had been angry, aggressive and oppositional as a toddler. His parents had always felt that he was bright but had never achieved his true potential, whereas the school regarded them as over-anxious, pushy parents. Once he started school he had increasingly become angry and defiant, his self-esteem had lowered and he became demoralised and continued to struggle with relationships.

Even the cat was scared of him, having been often thrown downstairs, chased, hit and had its fur cut off. His parents had to put a lock on the hamsters' cage when he was younger because he would squeeze and torment them. He was constantly destructive at home and in the garden. He was obsessed by flames and matches – once he set fire to the bin in the playground, and on another occasion he set light to some books and almost burned the house down.

At puberty he started to drink heavily and was intermittently involved in drug-taking. He tended to mix with similar types of boys and friendships did not last long. In class, he was disruptive, spoke out of turn, put up his hand without knowing the answer and generally clowned around. His speech was unclear, his concentration was poor and his reports always commented on his poor concentration and easy distractibility. His teachers said, 'He is great at arguing but has zero logic'.

Assessment

He had an average IQ score, but his reading, writing, spelling and mathematics were at age 8–9 levels, suggesting that he had an associated specific learning difficulty. Apart from clearly having AD/HD, he also had Oppositional Defiant Disorder, Conduct Disorder, speech and learning problems and intermittent depression.

Management

1. Methylphenidate improved concentration and impulsivity. However, he remained very oppositional.
2. Because of this and because of the sleep problems, after three months clonidine was added. This helped improve oppositionality and sleep and there was a great improvement in his overall wellbeing.
3. In parallel with this, supportive counselling and coaching was instituted, and he was given help with time management. He found he was no longer dependent on drugs and alcohol.
4. A Statement of Special Educational Needs was processed rapidly, he was placed in a pupil referral unit, and gradually, over six months, reintegrated to mainstream school.
5. He had help in a small group for social skills and gradually he discarded his old group of friends and developed more lasting friendships.

CASE NOTES	Sonia

Combined AD/HD, ODD, Conduct Disorder, anxiety and pregnancy

History

Sonia, aged 15, had a long-standing history of hyperactivity. She was adopted at three weeks and was extremely oppositional and antisocial by age 8. She had been expelled from several schools, had frequent difficulties with the youth justice system and had been placed in a pupil referral unit. She also tended to be very anxious, to have phobias and panic attacks and her self-esteem was extremely poor. She experimented with drug-taking, had many undesirable friends and her parents had been extremely concerned, feeling that every strategy had failed, and did not know what to do.

She frequently spent weekends in a social services respite home. There, one of the care workers felt that she may have AD/HD and suggested that her parents explore this further.

Assessment

Sonia clearly had AD/HD with many complications, including Oppositional Defiant Disorder and Conduct Disorder.

Management

1. A trial of methylphenidate was undertaken and she improved dramatically. However, she remained anxious and oppositional and within three months of starting methylphenidate she became pregnant.

2. Methylphenidate was ceased during the early part of the pregnancy as effects on the foetus are not fully known, and then continued later on. The labour was uneventful and a normal baby girl was born, who is developing well.

3. Sonia copes well with the baby, finds that she very much needs to take her methylphenidate to cope and has been helped by the addition of a low dose of antidepressant because of panic attacks and excessive anxiety. Her teachers had always felt that she was extraordinarily bright and she subsequently went back to college, achieved two As and a B at A-level and is now thinking about entering the legal profession.

What teachers can do

It is easy to underestimate how uncomfortable school can be for a child with AD/HD. A child who cannot sit still, cannot remember what has just been said, cannot copy accurately from the board and who finds it difficult to make and keep friends can find school a hostile place. Such a child's wonderful qualities and creativity may get lost in the struggle. Academic underachievement, behavioural problems and socialising difficulties, together with coexisting problems such as specific learning difficulties, depression or anxiety, may further complicate the situation. Children with AD/HD have a wide range of difficulties, and no two pupils will be the same; thus there can be a wide range of needs within the classroom.

For some children the main problems are with relative academic achievement, but this may be masked if the child has an above-average IQ. For others the behavioural difficulties are more of a problem – they will push the boundaries, violate classroom rules, call out in class and be increasingly disruptive. For some children, socialising difficulties affect their free time and ability to form friendships. These difficulties may fluctuate, so that the learning difficulties may be more of a problem at some times and the behaviour problems at others. The impulsiveness of AD/HD may be expressed both physically and, as a child gets older, more verbally. This impulsiveness frequently impedes effective social interaction.

A comprehensive educational and medical specialist assessment is essential for a diagnosis of AD/HD to be made. This assessment will determine *whether or not* AD/HD is present, and also identify any coexisting conditions.

The main strategies that have been scientifically evaluated to be effective in children with AD/HD are the use of medication and the use of behavioural modification, both in the classroom and in the home. Effective school strategies are always essential in the management of any child with AD/HD, whether or not medication is used. It is important for teachers to have a factual understanding of AD/HD so that they can implement effective behavioural strategies appropriate to the child.

Teachers also need to understand the role of medication as part of the treatment of AD/HD. The use of medication should never be seen as an 'either/or' situation. Medication stabilises the situation, lengthens the concentration span, helps with impulse control and lessens hyperactivity, i.e. treats the core AD/HD symptoms, and thus allows educational and behavioural management strategies to be more effective.

> The most effective strategies in managing children with AD/HD are medication and behavioural modification.

> For more on medication, see Chapter 4.

Common misconceptions about AD/HD

Teachers may encounter some of the following misconceptions about AD/HD:

- 'If he tried harder to concentrate I am sure he could do it.'
  AD/HD presents in a number of ways. In the inattentive form there are usually no behavioural problems, but children have relative difficulty in concentrating, especially on more mundane tasks. No matter how hard they try to concentrate, they simply cannot do it. Such children may be seen as 'lazy'.

- 'He can concentrate on computers and other interesting things for hours, but when he tries to do his homework he is up and down all the time.'
  There is a common misconception in educational circles that concentration is an 'all or nothing' situation. It has been clearly shown that many children, especially if they are bright, are able to over-focus on subjects which they find interesting, but are just unable to concentrate on other tasks. While everyone is like this to some extent, it is very marked in children with AD/HD.

- 'I don't believe in AD/HD – I think it's just an excuse for poor parenting.'
  AD/HD is not a religion; it is not the prerogative of an individual to believe in it or not. It is a clearly validated, internationally recognised condition that has been acknowledged in the UK by the National Institute for Clinical Excellence (NICE) in their reports in 2000 and 2005. It is a very real and debilitating condition, which is much more common than is generally recognised and can be responsible for long-standing academic, behavioural and social underachievement.

- 'I have seen a child who is subdued or almost a zombie on medication and I don't think children should be on it.'
  While a small percentage of children who are treated medically for AD/HD can become subdued, it is unusual for this to be the case once there has been careful fine-tuning and adjustment of dosage. In addition, the longer-acting preparations have made this side-effect less likely to occur.

AD/HD is a disability

It is helpful for teachers to have a 'disability perspective' and to recognise that AD/HD is a neuro-psychological disability of brain function. Children with AD/HD have difficulty in achieving the tasks that most people take for granted. It therefore means that accommodations, rather than excuses, need to be made in order to help children achieve to their often very considerable ability. An Individual Education Plan (IEP) for a child with significant problems can be very helpful. Some children may warrant a Statement of Special Educational Needs. However, this is usually unnecessary unless there are significant complicating factors. The majority of children with relatively uncomplicated AD/HD cope well in a mainstream situation with accommodations.

Historically, concentration difficulties tend to have been viewed under the same umbrella as dyslexia and dyspraxia. Nowadays it is recognised that many conditions of neuro-developmental dysfunction coexist, which means that many children with specific learning difficulties, such as dyslexia and dyspraxia, may also have difficulties with the core AD/HD symptoms of inattentiveness, impulsiveness or hyperactivity. Medical treatment of a child's AD/HD, so that he or she is able to concentrate, frequently creates a flow-on improvement in learning or co-ordination difficulties and the therapies for the problems are much more effective.

A child with AD/HD may:

- find it difficult to keep up with academic demands;
- need a great deal of support to stay on task and not be distracted;
- be inattentive and thus be poor at following classroom instructions;
- procrastinate and have difficulty following through with tasks and be inconsistent.

All of this can result in a greatly decreased volume of work being done. For other children with AD/HD, the verbal impulsiveness may mean that there is frequent calling out in class, and physical impulsiveness may mean other children being hit or punched, or things flicked across the room. High energy levels may also be problematic in the classroom. Frequent complications of: difficulties in organisation; planning and time management; and problems with motor planning, co-ordination and specific learning difficulties may also influence the situation.

Many children with AD/HD, who are untreated, become increasingly demoralised; their self-esteem decreases with the struggles they have to face, and they may become depressed or excessively anxious and frustrated. Other children demonstrate aspects of an autistic spectrum disorder, are excessively disruptive, or may have associated emotional and behavioural problems if there are issues within the family, e.g. marital, financial or environmental.

Accommodating AD/HD

The general characteristics of a school that is likely to be suitable for a child with AD/HD include:

- an understanding that such children will show a wide range of behaviours and have different learning styles;
- an informed, whole-school approach to the concept of specific learning difficulties, and especially an understanding of AD/HD – an awareness of its existence and its importance, rather than a sceptical approach;
- the ability to liaise closely between home, school and, where medication is used, medical professionals;
- an understanding that AD/HD is not an excuse, but rather an explanation for troublesome behaviours;
- where medication is used, an informed understanding of the rationale behind the use of medication, and also that additional strategies will probably be needed;
- a calm, encouraging and consistent approach, with a well-structured routine and clear rules. Closed-plan rooms, rather than an open and less structured environment, are more appropriate;
- a good extra-curricular programme;
- a mechanism for protecting and nurturing a child's self-esteem;
- screening children who might have emotional, behavioural or educational difficulties at an early age. This should be done as early as possible to prevent progression and before self-esteem, social skills and academic underachievement become problematic;
- the relevant teacher or SENCO must be in a position to screen and discuss any concerns with parents and, if necessary, to instigate basic educational,

academic and behavioural management. This is especially relevant if there is a long wait for a referral or an educational psychology assessment.

The transfer from primary to senior school can be quite problematic for children with AD/HD, especially if there are organisational and planning issues. In addition, obtaining feedback from a range of teachers regarding the child's subsequent progress can be more difficult.

A whole-school approach

Teachers can have a great influence on the general approach to school organisation, curriculum development and personal liaison with parents and other professionals involved with the child. The changes in attitude and understanding must involve the whole school, not just the SENCO. The dinner ladies, school administrative staff and indeed everyone who is involved in the school should have an understanding of the nature of AD/HD and its implications.

Teaching style

A teacher who believes in a child, who understands that child's strengths and weaknesses and who nurtures his or her self-esteem is very well placed to positively influence the child's life and is a very valuable asset.

However, the pressure on teachers of managing children with severe AD/HD can be quite significant. Teachers themselves need support and the ability to talk to other informed staff, to be trained in AD/HD and related problems and to feel confident in the way in which they are handling the child.

Teaching strategies for AD/HD

Removing Barriers to Achievement: Strategies for SEN, produced by the Department for Education and Skills and available online at *www.teachernet. gov.uk/senstrategy* gives more advice on practical teaching strategies for children with AD/HD.

Many theories of AD/HD consider that there is a core deficit in inhibition, which directly impacts on other areas, particularly those assisting self-regulation, short-term memory and sequencing. Providing inhibition delay (through medication) allows other executive functions to take place. Other theories consider that inhibition is not of prime importance, but that the problem is in executive functions – in the way in which the various skills are put together – like an orchestra without a conductor.

Among children with AD/HD, individual reaction to reinforcement and punishment depends on the level of motivation, the interest level and the different degrees of reinforcement and punishment. Recent research at the Learning Assessment & Neurocare Centre (LANC) in Sussex confirms what many teachers have known for a long time: the ability to concentrate and to inhibit inappropriate behaviours seems to be context-dependent – many children with AD/HD exhibit few such problems when playing computer games. The LANC research shows that inhibitory performance and on-task activity of children with AD/HD can be improved when tasks are made more interesting and, in particular, more 'computer

game-like'. The addition of narrative, rewards, response costs and colourful charac-
ters made a very significant difference to children's ability to concentrate and to be
better inhibited.

These studies suggest that in order to increase the chances of a child with AD/HD
maintaining attention and concentration, and of withholding impulsive responses
and inappropriate behaviours, the child needs to be sufficiently motivated and
stimulated with a combination of facilitating features and reinforcement strategies.
The use of computers appears to be very important and to impact significantly on
a child's interests, motivation, stimulation and, thus, level of achievement.

AD/HD teaching strategies

- **Teaching should be interactive, innovative, fun and motivating, without over-stimulating the child with AD/HD.**
  Teaching strategies should involve as many senses as possible. Small subtle changes of
  approach can make the difference between success and failure. Empathy, a sense of humour,
  patience, believing in the child and the ability to remain unflappable are important.

- **Set boundaries and limits for the child, both in the classroom and playground.**
  These should be clear, concise and constantly reinforced with limited choices. Have rules
  written down and regularly point out guidelines and limits. Children then understand exactly
  where they stand. Make clear what is acceptable and what is not. Have regular daily and weekly
  routines and forewarn the child of any changes. The use of contracts, lists and reminders may
  also be helpful.

  'Being fair' does not necessarily require that all children are treated identically. Rules and
  expectations may need to be individualised, but should be applied fairly and consistently. This
  does not mean that children with AD/HD should not be accountable for their actions; they
  should have to comply with the rules, which have been tailored to their needs, and be able to
  achieve what is expected of them. The threat of punishment actually has very little influence in
  deterring the child from breaking the rule, since their understanding of cause and effect is poor.

- **Classroom setting is important.**
  Open-plan classrooms pose considerable problems for children with AD/HD, allowing them to
  be easily distracted. The child with AD/HD needs to be seated near the front of the room, in a
  position where the distractions can be minimised, close to the teacher and, if possible, another
  pupil who would be a good role model. Increasing the distance between desks may also
  minimise distraction. Children with AD/HD perform better in a small class or a one-to-one
  situation.

- **Instructions should be repeated if necessary and given clearly and frequently.**
  Face the children, make eye contact first and keep instructions as concise, brief and clear as
  possible. Give one instruction at a time to avoid overwhelming the child. Instructions may
  need to be repeated and rules written down. State consequences clearly and fairly.

  Develop a private signal or cue for the child to start on a task, or other strategies. Positive
  instructions, such as 'put your feet on the floor' rather than 'don't put your feet on the desk'
  will have more effect. Make it clear that it is the behaviour that is not acceptable, not the child.
  Don't give instructions until the class is quiet and everyone is listening. Many children with
  AD/HD have problems with auditory instructions and, if dyslexic, may also have problems
  with visual instructions. Therefore, write the key points down as well as discussing them.
  Check that the instructions or topic have been understood.

■ **Give support to help concentration.**

Try and teach as much academic work as possible during the periods when the child is most likely to be concentrating. Break tasks into small, interesting segments. Try and alternate high- and low-interest tasks. This will also help their need for short-term achievements. Intersperse academic work with periods of exercise. Increase their allowable reasons to move. Sometimes, allowing a child an 'escape', such as delivering a message to another class, will help the child focus better on his/her return, without breaking the rules of leaving his/her seat without permission.

One-to-one tuition through a non-teaching assistant, parent or peer may also help poor concentration. Frequent eye contact is extremely useful for the child who is daydreaming and a perceptive teacher can make very effective use of the glance.

■ **Praise and reward appropriate behaviour and achievements.**

Give immediate and frequent feedback, and as much immediate reinforcement as possible. Try to ignore minor misbehaviour. This will help make the child with AD/HD feel motivated and inspired, rather than defeated. Access to privileges and/or responsibility are frequently very motivating rewards. Children with AD/HD have tremendous difficulty working towards long-term goals and respond much better to repeated reinforcement and encouragement. Despite their difficulties, children with AD/HD are often very creative and have special skills. They cannot be over-praised for effort and good behaviour. Frequently, a huge amount of effort has gone into a task, especially homework. This effort should be recognised, even if some of the work is substandard.

Try to minimise any attention to their weaknesses and teach tolerance. Discovering, highlighting and nurturing their areas of competence can be a very positive way of improving self-esteem, behaviour and social skills within the peer group. By the time they have struggled at school for a year or two, they almost always see themselves as failing and have fragile self-esteem. The teacher's attitude towards the child in front of their peers counts for a great deal.

■ **Structure, routine, predictability and consistency.**

Change should be foreshadowed, rules should be consistent and routine adhered to. Loss of structure at lunchtime can aggravate behavioural difficulties.

■ **Reprimand or punish very carefully.**

Use careful reprimands for misbehaviour rather than appearing stressed, losing control, lecturing, ridiculing or excessively criticising the child in front of the class. If mistakes and errors are made, teach the child ways of using them in a positive way for future learning, rather than seeing the child as a failure. Be aware of the child's hypersensitivity, especially if his/her self-esteem is low. Teaching a child to think before acting and to become aware of the consequences of his or her actions with prompts such as '1, 2, 3' or 'Stop, Think, Do' is essential. Act quickly to intervene with inappropriate behaviour. If possible, deal with it and move on quickly to a more positive area. The '1, 2, 3' strategies are particularly useful for younger children, as is using 'time out'. Avoid removing activities that the child does well, just for the sake of discipline. The child's confidentiality should be respected and any special arrangements for medication or modification of expected class standards of achievement should not be made common knowledge.

■ **Behavioural report cards.**

After each lesson, write a comment or give a mark out of ten for the child's behaviour. Reward a series of positive comments.

- **Foreshadow/be aware of potentially problematic situations.**
  Unstructured situations such as playtime often cause problems for children with AD/HD. They may have trouble reading social cues, body language, voice tone etc. They may be isolated in the playground or always at the centre of trouble, because of their over-reaction to the stimulus and their impulsive behaviour. Giving guidelines on what to do during playtime can be useful. Transitions need regular routine and forewarning.

  Extra time may be necessary for processing and completing tasks. Organisational problems should be addressed and discussed. Just writing things down might take a huge effort. Encourage the use of lists to help organise the day – diaries, timetables and report cards are all helpful. Many of the strategies mentioned above will help with organisation and time management, especially lists, prioritising and planning for assignments.

- **Ask the child for his/her ideas.**
  Children often have some very definite ideas of how they feel they could cope better and what strategies might help. It can be very helpful, and at times humbling, to talk to them about these.

- **Protect and enhance self-esteem.**
  Many behaviours associated with AD/HD may have a significant impact on a child's self-esteem. Protecting it and enhancing it through the school years is a crucial goal of effective management. Strategies should help children succeed by virtue of their own efforts, so that the child's courage, individual strengths and positive qualities can be focused upon, while their vulnerabilities may be noted. Children with low self-esteem need to feel that they are not isolated or worthless, but that they are contributing to a larger group and are valued within it, because people listen, care and share. Teachers should clarify that it is the misbehaviour, not the child, which is unacceptable. Ways of praising or reprimanding the child (see above) must demonstrate belief in him/her.

- **Support social skills difficulties.**
  The child's name may well have gone before him/her because of impulsive, aggressive or inappropriate behaviour. It takes time for this to be rectified and needs support.

- Children with AD/HD often test the limits of teachers and parents. In order to help the child you need to remain in control and respond positively, not allowing yourself to get drawn into a negative behavioural style.

- **Assess situations with the AD/HD child in mind.**
  School trips or a school play are likely to make the child very excited. Establish one or two essential rules before the event, and make sure the child knows what the rules are and what will happen if she/he does or does not comply. It may be necessary to plan for a parent or classroom assistant to be present at the event.

- **Create an organised educational environment.**
  Make sure the classroom is well-organised, tidy and calm; teach children how to organise their desk, time etc.; establish and display a daily routine; develop a clear system for keeping track of completed/uncompleted work; provide due dates for all assignments and make sure the child has copied them into his/her homework book.

- Be conscious of the hypersensitivity of AD/HD children to words, actions, situations, etc. They often over-react to triggers that appear minor to the observer.

- A child with AD/HD is usually about one-third less mature than his chronological age, with a 2–4-year lag in age-appropriate developmental skills – he knows what to do but does not always do what he knows.

Addressing coexisting features

As most children with AD/HD have a number of coexisting or complicating features, it is important to address these once the core AD/HD symptoms have been taken into account. Key among these coexisting problems are:

- Specific learning difficulties
  Support may involve using specific dyslexia-type programmes, one-to-one support to help with phonics, the use of computerised learning techniques, etc.

- Support for planning, organisation and time management
  These are executive function difficulties and frequently persist despite adequate treatment of the core AD/HD symptoms. Many children with AD/HD have a very poor concept of time and thus are often late and appear disorganised. These children benefit from help in time management, planning and organisation, and having an AD/HD coach can be very helpful here. Colour-co-ordinated folders, having a school–home diary, strategies for remembering homework, planning the days and week ahead etc. are essential here.

- Disruptive Behavioural Disorder
  This includes those children with Oppositional Defiant Disorder and Oppositional Defiant Disorder and Conduct Disorder. Children with this condition have persistent behavioural difficulties despite being managed effectively for their AD/HD. They need very strict behavioural and educational strategies, and at times may be helped by the use of additional medications to try to mellow their disruptive behavioural disorder difficulties.

- Ongoing emotional and behavioural difficulties
  If these result from family issues, specific counselling/psychological therapies may be helpful. For example, in a child who has AD/HD and attachment difficulties emanating from issues relating to adoption and/or earlier abuse, specific counselling is essential.

- Persistently low self-esteem or demoralisation
  This usually improves when the AD/HD is treated. However, if it does not, extra supports may be necessary. Some children with these issues are more likely to be involved in bullying or self-harm.

- Autistic spectrum features
  These may include poor social communication, over-focused interests, lack of empathy or poor eye contact. There is a range of autistic spectrum difficulties, the commonest of which in this context is Asperger's Syndrome. Autistic spectrum difficulties can coexist with AD/HD, and the extent of their impact on a child is often hard to assess until the child's AD/HD symptoms and other medically treatable conditions have been managed effectively.

- Developmental Co-ordination Disorder (DCD)/dyspraxia/DAMP/disorders of attention and motor perception
  Up to 50 per cent of children with AD/HD also have a DCD. Poor motor co-ordination affects many aspects of school life – slowness of dressing, changing for sports, sports themselves and interaction on the playground. It is also seen in the classroom as the 'clumsy child' bumps into things, knocks over his/her

chair and fails to clap in rhythm to the school song. The most common problem seen in the classroom is with handwriting. Research shows that children with both AD/HD and DCD have a psycho-socially poorer outcome than those with AD/HD alone. They need special attention, which usually involves treating the AD/HD appropriately and then providing appropriate remedial attention for learning and co-ordination difficulties.

For example, if a child is still having considerable problems with handwriting, a paediatric occupational therapy assessment should be sought to ascertain which of the skill areas mentioned above are deficient. Suitable strategies can then be planned to support classroom learning. These may involve strategies to improve the child's sensory integration. This is a specialised therapy that builds on the child's sensory experience, which in turn can improve both motor and academic performance. Other children will need help with their visual perceptual skills (how the brain interprets what the eye sees), their visual motor skills (how the hand and eyes work together) or their fine motor skills (how their hands work). Some work is done directly with the child, and some by the suggestion of strategies for use at home or school.

Problems with handwriting

A child who is asked to manipulate a pencil before he or she has the necessary control of the movements of the finger joints may, typically, hold forcefully onto the pencil for stability (frequently breaking the lead) and write using the movements of the whole hand. This fisted grip means of holding the pencil initially helps to overcome the child's problems, but this may become a habit and the child may continue to use it even when they have the maturation and ability to use their finger joints. The result is often immature writing and a painful hand.

Handwriting is a complicated learning task: the child has to have mastered certain levels of visual-perceptual, visual-motor, gross and fine motor skills. They must have adequate sensori-motor foundations, motor planning and spatial awareness. On top of this they must have the cognitive and language ability to organise ideas, express them appropriately and understand the rules of grammar and syntax. All of this assumes that they have been able to pay attention and learn the skill as taught by the teacher.

The three Ps of handwriting
- POSTURE
  Make sure that the child has a chair and table/desk that is appropriate. His/her feet should be on the floor; ankles, knees, hips and elbows should be as close to right angles as possible. Good posture provides the stability to the child's body that can then allow the mobility of the hand. A slightly sloped writing surface encourages extension at the wrists and improves dexterity. This can be accomplished by attaching the child's exercise book to a closed two- or three-inch ring binder with the raised edge away from the child. A piece of non-slip rubber mat on the bottom prevents the file from moving about on the desk.

■ PAPER

This needs to be positioned correctly so that the child can see what he or she is writing. Imagine the child sitting with both elbows on the desk with hands together so that they form a right angle – the right-handed child should align the top of the paper with the left arm in this position and the left-handed child should align it with the right arm. A piece of masking tape on the desk to remind child and teacher of the paper position can be useful. This is extremely important for left-handed students who frequently develop a 'hooked hand' when writing on poorly positioned paper, in order to see what they are writing. The paper needs to be of good enough quality that writing is a pleasing experience, whatever implement is used.

■ PENCIL/PEN

This needs to be a good quality tool that works for the child. A pencil with a larger shaft is easier to manipulate. The younger child will need repeated prompting to hold the pencil with the 'proper grip'. The important aspect of the grip is that there is a space between the thumb and the first finger so that the pencil can be moved by the thumb and first finger in opposition to each other, with the second finger providing support under the pencil. If the space between the thumb and first finger is closed, as in a child fisting the hand around the pencil, then increasing the size of the pencil shaft should help. The shaft can be increased by using a pencil grip or by taping three pencils together with the writing one slightly longer than the other two. A felt-tip handwriting pen may be easier for a child with a heavy grip who frequently breaks pencil leads. The best quality coloured pencils, markers or crayons should be used to minimise the frustration experience for the child.

Correcting pencil grips: once the child has habituated a less-than-functional grip (usually by the age of 7), it is very hard to change. However, many go on to write successfully with very strange grips that may well cause problems in later life, but which are adequate in these days of computers.

Computers are often the long-term answer to illegible handwriting, but learning keyboard skills can be just as frustrating for a child as they require good fine motor and motor planning skills. Until a student can type at a minimum of 20 words per minute, using a computer is no less frustrating than using a pencil. A good typing programme for the computer used regularly, little and often (e.g. 15 minutes, five times a week) is the most effective method of learning. A reward system built in by the parents to give immediate rewards for successful participation with the programme will be the most effective method. Generally, a laptop computer for a student with AD/HD in the classroom is an expensive risk and an added distraction. Cheaper solutions are available such as the portable word processor, the AlphaSmart (www.AlphaSmart.com) or similar.

Other classroom accommodations include:

■ Modifying the amount that the AD/HD and DCD student needs to write

Creative solutions include involving other students as note-takers, allowing the student to dictate answers, using speech-enabled computer software. Teachers have to balance the need to know what the child knows with insisting on the written word being the only way to express this knowledge. Typically, the child who has problems with handwriting is very aware of their lack of skill and will try to avoid it. The risk is that they have a paragraph of knowledge in their heads but are only prepared to put a sentence on paper. Like all aspects of learning, a sense of success builds self-confidence and encourages new learning. The challenge for the teacher is to find a way for poor writers to feel successful, while encouraging them to improve.

The importance of understanding AD/HD

It has been well documented that in special schools, such as those for children with emotional and behavioural difficulties, there is a much higher incidence of AD/HD, often complicated by coexisting conditions and by environmental difficulties.

It is simply not possible to maintain effective educational services without identification and effective management of children with neurobiological difficulties, especially AD/HD and autistic spectrum difficulties. The contribution these children make to excessive problems with disruptive behavioural disorders, exclusions, the need for extra schooling support, educational underachievement and, in some cases, entry into the criminal justice system is vast and highly preventable.

> In the USA the law dictates that prior to a child being permanently suspended or excluded from school there must be an assessment to ascertain whether or not the child has AD/HD, autistic spectrum difficulty or some similar neuro-biological difficulty that may have contributed to the child's exclusion. Although not law in the UK, it would seem sensible for a similar approach to be taken.

Troubleshooting in the classroom

For some children additional strategies are necessary over and above the more basic management strategies for a child with AD/HD. Below are some common classroom scenarios, with suggestions for strategies that may be helpful for teachers.

The diagnosis of AD/HD has been made in a child, but there are persistent difficulties with impulsive behavioural comments or actions and poor concentration.

If medication is not being used, it is possible that it should be. If it is, then dosage or timing adjustments should be made. Teacher feedback to the child's parents and doctor/specialist is essential in order to develop the optimum dosage regime.

The core AD/HD symptoms are well contained, but there are persistent problems with planning, organisation and time management.

The best strategy is to try to minimise the impact of a child's disorganisation on his/her schooling and life difficulties. Specific strategies – such as working with the home, having home–school diaries, foreshadowing situations, colour-coding books etc. – are necessary here. Having a coach or mentor can also be very helpful.

The child's AD/HD core symptoms are satisfactorily controlled, but there is still difficulty in writing things down.

Consider whether there may be associated developmental co-ordination difficulties or problems with co-ordination and visual processing. An occupational therapist might help. Sometimes the difficulty in writing things down is due to boredom . . . ('Why should I write it down if I can say it straight away?') and sometimes due to short-term memory issues. Frequently, improving typing skills and then working on the computer is helpful in this situation.

Concentration improves but there are still problems with short-term memory.

Usually, additional changes in medication will not make a great deal of difference and it is important that tight educational strategies be implemented, utilising the best means of processing information for the child, i.e. visual or auditory.

The child can concentrate on Lego, computers and other things of interest, but will not, or cannot, concentrate on the subjects which are less interesting.

Anyone can concentrate better on things that are interesting, but AD/HD children seem to have a faulty 'on–off switch' and are unable to switch on for the less interesting subjects. Generally, adjustments to medication can be helpful in this situation. It is important not to extrapolate and assume that because a child is able to concentrate on interesting subjects that he or she should then be able to concentrate on anything.

The child's core AD/HD symptoms are well contained, but there is persistent oppositionality, arguing, defying and pushing the boundaries of school discipline.

Consider whether the child may have associated Oppositional Defiant Disorder. This is usually, but not always, more of a problem in the home rather than in the school, but it would be worth asking parents about this. In many cases, when the core AD/HD symptoms are treated, the Oppositional Defiant Disorder symptoms and Conduct Disorder symptoms also improve. However, there are many children where this does not happen, and if reasonable behavioural strategies have not been effective there is an increasing tendency to use a second, additional medication to try to mellow the oppositionality. Generally, self-esteem and social skills will not improve until this is done.

Despite adequate treatment, self-esteem remains low and motivation poor, and the child continues to be demoralised.

Consider whether the core AD/HD symptoms are, in fact, adequately treated. If so, then consider whether the child might be depressed or have other complications or environmental difficulties that are not being fully addressed. Sometimes it becomes more apparent with time that there is evidence of associated autistic spectrum difficulties coexisting with the child's AD/HD, i.e. difficulty in socialising appropriately, lack of eye contact, lack of empathy and/or ritualistic or obsessive behaviours. Also consider whether the child's environment could be more supportive and nurturing and whether the child's 'islets of competence' are being satisfactorily sought and rewarded.

The classroom situation is satisfactory but there are problems at playtime and at lunchtime.

Consider whether medication may be wearing off in the unstructured times. Consider also whether, prior to diagnosis and treatment, a child's name may have gone before him/her due to when they were more impulsive or oppositional. If it is considered that the child's AD/HD is managed effectively, consider using a play buddy, investigate the possibility of bullying and try to find playground activities that might hold the child's interest.

The child's AD/HD appears to be adequately treated but he/she continues to learn at a relatively slow rate.

Consider whether an Educational Psychology evaluation would be helpful. It is useful to know what expectations are reasonable for a child: is he or she of high or low IQ? Are there any coexisting specific learning difficulties? In most cases this will already have been appraised at the initial assessment, but the profile of the child can change once AD/HD is managed effectively. Children with AD/HD and specific learning difficulties need support for both problems, and the child may well need specific support for his/her dyslexia or other learning difficulty.

The child appears to be sad, miserable and possibly depressed, despite the AD/HD being treated.

Discuss the situation with the parents and consider whether there are any other issues at school such as bullying or unidentified learning difficulties that may be impacting on the situation. If the sadness continues then the child's medical practitioner might wish to consider whether an antidepressant should be prescribed. Occasionally, manic depression (bipolar disorder) can coexist with AD/HD. In the more inattentive-only form of AD/HD, which occurs especially in girls, depression is a frequent coexisting condition.

It is considered that the child might have AD/HD, but the parents are not at all interested in this possibility.

Try to explain to the parents exactly what difficulties you are seeing in the classroom; encourage them to become better informed on AD/HD and related difficulties and to ignore the myth and misinformation which has been so prevalent in the lay press. Explain that you consider that the child has potential but is underachieving and/or has behavioural or other difficulties that might be consistent with AD/HD. It is important that concerns about treatment do not obscure the route to diagnosis.

The child is gifted but underachieving relative to ability.

Consider whether the child is bored and is not being challenged sufficiently. Consider whether the fact that the child can concentrate on the interesting subjects, but not on the boring ones, might mean that he or she is being under-treated medically. Help from the National Association for Able Students might be useful, as might a recognition of the child's true ability, and measures put in place to try to achieve these.

As a teacher, you feel you are doing all you can for a child and yet things are still not working out.

Develop a dialogue with the medical practitioner treating the child so that, together with the parents, you can make decisions about why things are not working out. Problems may arise from:

- insufficient doses of medication;
- the lack of use of an additional medication to treat complications such as depression or Oppositional Defiant Disorder;
- a lack of understanding of the basic nature of AD/HD and thus a less than adequate implementation of teaching strategies;
- the fact that the child has persistent planning, organisation and time management difficulties which will probably not respond to additional medications.

7 The long-term outlook

AD/HD creates a significant vulnerability and makes the person more likely to experience difficulties later in life. Such difficulties include academic under-achievement, difficulties with peer relationships and family functioning, low self-esteem, difficulties with employment and occupations, and increased difficulty with mood and anxiety disorders. For some, especially those who have disruptive and antisocial difficulties early in life, there is an increased incidence of entry to the criminal justice system and substance abuse.

However, the wide range of presentations of people with AD/HD, the variability in coexisting conditions and the differing environments have made it very difficult to judge the outcome for any one particular person with AD/HD. It is also difficult to know to what degree effective management helps people with AD/HD. There are, however, a number of studies now – mostly on the shorter term – which, combined with wide clinical experience, indicate that many features of AD/HD can be helped effectively; and the long-term outlook for the majority of people who are treated in a finely managed way can be a great deal better than if that person is not treated at all.

The initial management aim for anyone of school age with AD/HD is to enable them to get through their school years as intact as possible. This means that, at the very minimum, the child's self-esteem, academic and social skills must be protected so that he or she finishes school doing as well as possible in these areas. Frequently, once someone with AD/HD has found a career pathway that interests them, what in the past has been a problem or a handicap can become a very positive characteristic.

Some children with AD/HD appear to outgrow it by the end of their school years, especially if they are diagnosed and treated early. The majority benefit from medication during their school years; as adults they may be unable to concentrate on boring subjects or might still be impulsive, but usually their lives are much better, either on or off medication, than if they had not been treated. Nowadays, adult AD/HD is widely recognised as being a valid condition, and there is no doubt that in at least 70 per cent of cases significant AD/HD symptoms persist into adulthood.

As with the medical treatment of any condition, the long-term use of any medication needs to be monitored constantly and any concerns about side-effects must be balanced against benefits obtained. AD/HD is not a static condition and, unfortunately, progresses, untreated, with time. Children should always be under constant professional review, and regular decisions should be made on whether or not the benefits of medication warrant continuation of treatment.

The multi-modal treatment study undertaken by the MTA Cooperative Group of the National Institute of Mental Health (NIMH) in the United States, published in 1999, looked at the outcomes of treating children with AD/HD in four different ways. The results are now available for a two-year period. The children were divided

Treating AD/HD in children aims to protect their self-esteem, academic and social skills, enabling them to achieve their potential at school.

Clinical experience shows that with careful long-term management, almost all children with AD/HD of a wide range of presentations and severity can be helped.

into: (a) a group that received intensive medication management only; (b) a group where intensive medication management was combined with intensive behavioural, educational and social skills therapy; (c) a third group where behavioural therapy alone was used; and (d) a fourth group where the care was on a rather *ad hoc* basis in the local community.

The results showed that in all four groups it was possible to show an improvement in AD/HD symptoms. However, the groups where medication was used intensively showed the most significant reduction, not only in core AD/HD symptoms but also in many other areas. While there is no doubt that behavioural therapy adds to the overall improvement in self-esteem and social skills in many children with AD/HD, especially if there are complications, it would appear that if there is significant AD/HD, the use of carefully tuned medication is the most important management arm, especially so that the child can be more available for educational and learning strategies.

> Carefully controlled studies on the treatment of AD/HD show clear improvement in behaviour and learning with a decrease in overactivity.

In the UK, a recent study from the Bedford Group for Life Courses and Statistical Studies looked at adult outcomes of AD/HD, using the 1970 British cohort following all children born in Great Britain in the first week of April 1970. It showed that those who had AD/HD at age 10 were significantly more likely than those without AD/HD to face a wide range of negative outcomes in adulthood, especially in the areas of social exclusion, education, economic status, housing, relationships, crime and health. It showed that men tended to fare less well and were specifically at greater risk of homelessness, more serious offending, being the victims of assault, having alcohol-related problems, obsessive life behaviour and having psychiatric disturbance by age 30. Women, on the other hand, were at greater risk of earning a low income, being a single parent and living in a workless household. Also, 2 per cent of the sample had not experienced any of the 24 negative outcomes, thus suggesting that there is a group of people with AD/HD who have a resilience to the problems it creates. This is borne out by clinical experience.

So far, no studies have investigated the long-term effects of having predominantly inattentive AD/HD. However, clinical experience shows that in a good environment, especially where the child has a reasonable IQ, such children usually respond to modest doses of medication, and most progress into adulthood fairly well, provided there are no associated severe learning, anxiety or depressive difficulties.

On the other hand, children with the more hyperactive symptoms – especially if there is the associated early onset of disruptive behaviour disorder – are at more risk, even with treatment, of having an adverse outcome. Having parents with untreated and significant AD/HD, where there are poor family relationships and inconsistent child-rearing habits, exacerbate a poor outcome. Similarly, living in an isolated family with continuing financial, housing or employment difficulties, and where there is little support from the

> The Bedford Group study found that men and women who had AD/HD at age 10 were more likely to be:
>
> ■ unqualified or with low levels of qualifications
>
> ■ living in a low socio-economic situation
>
> ■ living in a workless household
>
> ■ living in temporary accommodation
>
> ■ single, separated or divorced
>
> ■ cigarette smokers
>
> ■ dissatisfied with their lives
>
> ■ depressed or have drug problems.

school and others, exacerbates the outcome difficulties. However, factors that may improve the outcome include having milder core AD/HD symptoms, fewer complications, a higher IQ and being diagnosed earlier in life.

When the diagnosis of AD/HD is not made until teenage years, where the adolescent has progressed through puberty and has entered the more complex field of senior school, the outcome again appears to be worse. Then, the disruptive behaviour difficulties are often magnified, social skills difficulties make the progression into substance misuse or antisocial behaviour much more likely and increased demoralisation means it is frequently difficult to engage the adolescent in effective management.

People with the hyperactive form of AD/HD who have the early onset of disruptive behaviour disorder, especially if there is associated mood instability, are much more likely to enter the youth justice system. For this to have happened represents a failure on the part of educational and medical systems. It is not only tragic for a person with such a treatable condition to have been allowed to progress this far, but it is a reflection on society and the failure of these systems to have adequately protected the child. While adolescents within the youth justice system *can* still be treated for AD/HD, it is much more difficult, and the ravages of the environment are greatly increased by that stage.

Positive features of AD/HD

It is always important, however, to remember the positive attributes of the child. Parents almost always note their child's positive characteristics, which may have become blurred or lost by the AD/HD difficulties. With treatment, these positive attributes can be turned to the individual's advantage. It is therefore important to reframe the AD/HD once it is managed effectively. This is a very important part of management, especially in adolescence. The long-term educational, social, relationship and other goals often change to an extent not previously thought possible. Once a child with AD/HD is able to finish school and start on further education or employment in an area of interest, the ability to over-focus and be extremely energetic can lead to great success.

As adults, people with AD/HD have many adaptive characteristics. They tend to think across boundaries and devise new ways of doing things. Because they get bored easily, they tend not to stay with any one thing for very long. They are able

Table 7.1 Factors affecting the outlook for people with AD/HD (modified from Wall and Nash 1996)

	Supporting factors	Hindering factors
Children:	milder core symptoms few complications early diagnosis high IQ predominantly inattentive ADHD	severe core symptoms many complications late diagnosis low IQ early-onset ODD or CD Asperger's Syndrome
Parents:	AD/HD absent or resolved no psychiatric or social problems high IQ good family relationships child-rearing consistent and supportive	AD/HD unresolved psychiatric or social problems lower IQ poor family relationships
Environment:	supportive extended family no financial, employment or housing problems school co-operation and support	isolation from family financial, employment or housing problems no school support

to switch their attention from one thing to another, and often have many things on the go at one time. They tend to see things not noticed by others, and they are generally fairly intuitive. However, their disorganisation can make them appear somewhat chaotic. Working within conventional systems or rules is not always easy and often they will achieve goals by somewhat unconventional means.

Especially if adequately treated, adults with AD/HD can be delightful individuals with many endearing characteristics. However, untreated AD/HD wreaks havoc on the lives of many, and is responsible for a wide range of difficulties from relationship problems, dysfunctional families, drug and alcohol abuse and employment difficulties, to name a few.

> **Positive attributes in the workplace**
> Adults with AD/HD:
>
> - tend to think across boundaries
> - may be creative and work unconventionally
> - may be intuitive
> - often use their ability to over-focus to great advantage

CASE STUDY **Tom – A real-life story (written with Anne Douglas)**

The early years

As a toddler and a preschooler, Tom races through the surface of life like a runaway train, scattering people and objects as he goes. His energy levels are incredible. New toys, new people and new situations never satisfy him for long and everything is a battle. He never learns from his mistakes, has no sense of danger and bumps and bruises are the norm. The day always begins from the moment he is awake with his insatiable demands. No-one is prepared to babysit because he is so exhausting and it's no fun to take him anywhere. We wonder where we are going wrong.

His parents say:

- He never wants a cuddle.
- How can our lives be dictated to by such a small being?
- We just go from one crisis to another.

The health visitor says:

- He's not hyperactive because he sleeps all right.
- You really need to be firmer with him and not let him get away with so much.
- Try giving him a soothing bath at midnight, if he's active all evening.

The playgroup says:

- He's a real live wire and obviously only here for the social side of things.

Family friends say:

- Boys are like that, he'll grow out of it.

The GP says:

- He's just hyperactive; he'll grow out of it by puberty.
- I'll arrange counselling for you if you like.

The school years

By the time Tom goes to school his parents are reading all the parenting books they can get their hands on and are desperately trying to find better ways of dealing with him. Relationships are becoming very strained as he constantly confronts and defies the most reasonable efforts to improve his behaviour. Everyday tasks are a struggle. His hypersensitivity creates constant tension. He is over-competitive and possessive and regularly quarrels with his brother and friends.

His school reports poor concentration, laziness, easy distractibility and disorganisation and complains of class clowning and uncompleted homework and other tasks. However, they feel he has the potential to do better. They clearly expect his parents to improve the situation and they question their discipline.

Life becomes one long round of arguments and tantrums from morning till night. Tom is permanently volatile and easily gets angry. Everyday life and holidays have to be geared to his needs as, unless he is happy, no-one else gets any peace. His parents are at their wits' end to know where to turn for help, ashamed to admit that they do not know how to bring up their own son. His brother, whom they treat the same way, seems to behave more appropriately, but it is clear that Tom reacts differently in every situation.

His parents say:

- He is so single-minded, he almost doesn't seem to have a conscience.
- He uses 'No' all the time, but doesn't respond to it himself.
- He doesn't appreciate the effect his volatile actions have on the family.
- When he occasionally slows down long enough to communicate, you can see the lost soul beneath the layers of chaos.

His teachers say:

- He is just lazy, disorganised and forgetful.
- No amount of reward or punishment makes any difference.
- Tom doesn't seem to understand cause and effect.

His brother says:

- He tries to dominate everything – it's always his rules.

Family friends say:

- You're over-protective.

The years 18–24

Exam results were naturally disappointing as life progressively deteriorated for Tom. The lack of structure in further education led to poor attendance, incomplete work, missed deadlines and failed assignments. Disorganisation and chaos dominated his existence. Money slipped through his fingers as he endlessly sought new stimulation to beat the constant boredom he felt. His whole existence was a disaster and it was difficult to envisage any kind of future for him, yet he still resisted attempts to help. He went from job to job without direction, finding everything too boring and not being able to concentrate long enough to learn new things. Gradually, he realised that he was being left behind by his brother and friends, as they began new stages of their lives. However, there was one positive outcome to this catalogue of despondency: starting work forced him to acknowledge his own problems and, at last, he was motivated to take some action.

His parents say:

- His problems certainly didn't stop once he was a teenager, as the books said they would.
- He puts off everything till later.
- We can't really see him ever becoming really independent or mature.

His brother says:

- He leaves a trail of chaos; his bedroom has to be seen to be believed.
- It's hard to remember any good times we shared.
- My parents always had different rules for him – it wasn't fair.

His friends say:

- He loses interest in things so quickly.

His employers say:

- His timekeeping is appalling.
- He has had so many jobs already.

Now (age 25)

Although his parents realised eight years ago that he almost certainly had AD/HD, he would only accept advice recently and was only then formally diagnosed. The change in his demeanour has been remarkable since he embarked on the treatment for his AD/HD. He confided in his mother that he used to think he was a freak. The treatment has allowed him to be reflective for the first time and he is happier about himself as he now participates in his life instead of it controlling him. He says he feels more confident, enjoys being more responsible and is keen to get on with his life and make up for lost time. He now realises how much his inability to concentrate hindered him throughout school. Instead of criticism, accusation and rejection he now gets encouragement, praise and acceptance for his achievements, both at work and leisure. Previously, apart from his talent at football, his poor concentration, boredom and impulsiveness have prevented him from trying or accomplishing anything new.

He is motivated to continue with his treatment because he recognises that it works. There is no doubt that he clearly needs his medication. Both he and his family are acutely aware if he misses a dose or when they have worn off. The quality of his life is so much better and he can start to build on his successes.

For almost 25 years Tom's life had been utterly chaotic and distressing both to himself and those who care about him. Those outside the family who were involved with him had little time for his volatile, immature and unreasonable behaviour, yet underneath it all one sensed there was a lost soul, desperately trying to feel normal. His courage in finally confronting his problems and accepting the necessary help has unlocked a likeable and enthusiastic personality, with great potential. Of course, it will not all be plain sailing and there are bound to be setbacks. However, where once he had no future, at last he has the chance to fulfil his potential.

His GP said:

- This AD/HD thing is just an American fad.
- I've never heard of adult AD/HD.
- I wouldn't prescribe a dangerous medication anyway.

The specialist says:

- He has long-standing severe AD/HD. I can't understand why he hasn't even been treated for his hyperactivity before now. He also has ODD and OCD. The most effective help for him is medication and I would recommend an appropriate trial.

Tom says:

- I've never really known what it was like to concentrate before.
- I have so much to catch up on in my life to make up for lost time.
- I realise I never revised for exams because I just couldn't get started and it was too boring.
- I've now read my first book from cover to cover; before, I couldn't even take in the first line.
- I got my driving licence when I was 18 but never had the confidence to drive. Now I've started again.
- Work is going so well.
- I've got my first girlfriend.
- I'm able to try new things and am no longer afraid of failing.

His brother says:

- He is calmer and more interested in others.
- He is much better company and a real friend now.

His parents say:

- He is perceptive and thoughtful now; he even thinks about others and shows appreciation.
- We can see a future for him now; at last he has a chance of making the most of his opportunities and realising that he is, after all, lovable and effective.

Concluding comments

The existence of AD/HD is now well beyond debate. In the UK it was validated by the report of the National Institute of Clinical Excellence in 2000, and developed further with a review in 2004. The management of AD/HD is increasingly being incorporated into expectations of the Health Service by clinical governance, and also into the educational service, especially by the Children's National Service Framework and by the Government's strategy for special educational needs – *Removing Barriers to Achievement* (2004).

It is accepted that the condition is managed both by paediatricians and psychiatrists within child and adolescent mental health services; there is a need for closer integration between these services and educational services. There is now a general recognition that the condition is not just about severe hyperactivity but also about the broader concept of AD/HD, which includes inattentiveness and impulsiveness. The importance of comorbidity in determining clinical presentation and in predicting outcome is also respected.

There is also increased recognition and understanding of the reality of AD/HD, and commissioning of children's services increasingly acknowledges this. The earlier scepticism about the very existence of AD/HD and about the medications frequently used to treat it is gradually being replaced by an awareness of the importance of AD/HD in the special educational needs framework and in society generally. The pseudo-controversy largely caused by the myth and misinformation from those sceptical of AD/HD continues, but it is generally minimised.

There is still, however, a lot of progress to made in recognising the condition in adolescents and adults, and especially within the criminal justice system. The fact that a high percentage of people within the youth justice system have untreated AD/HD, and have progressed untreated through school, raises a great many issues regarding better provision of mental health services for the youth justice, and indeed, criminal justice systems.

There will always be much more to learn about AD/HD, but this should not detract from the reality of the condition, nor prevent us from applying the knowledge we already have to the effective treatment of adults and children. Children with AD/HD are not 'problem children' but children who have a problem. Unrecognised and untreated AD/HD prevents a happy childhood and blights a future.

The families of children with AD/HD deserve support and understanding, not blame. The increasing evidence that AD/HD is a biological deficit in impulse control, and thus in self- control, goes to the heart of commonly held societal beliefs of self-responsibility and is one of the main reasons for controversy surrounding AD/HD.

However, the effects of AD/HD need to be experienced to be truly understood. The condition deserves to be taken much more seriously. It is vital that all

> Studies suggest that between 50% and 70% of young people within the youth justice system may have untreated AD/HD.

> For more on the biological causes of AD/HD, see Appendix 2.

professionals involved with children be open-minded, become informed and acknowledge the existence and reality of AD/HD and their role in providing essential management and support. Children with AD/HD and their families should expect nothing less.

Appendix 1: Further reading

General

ADDISS (2003) *AD/HD – Parents, Provision and Policy – A Consultation with Parents* (www.addiss.co.uk).

Amen, D.G. (2001) *Healing ADD*. Berkley Publishing Group.

Barkley, R.A. (1998) *Attention Deficit Hyperactivity Disorder – A Handbook for Diagnosis and Treatment*. Guilford Press.

Barkley, R.A. (1998) *Taking Charge of ADHD: The Complete Authoritative Guide for Parents*. Guilford Press.

Brown, T. (2000) *Attention Deficit Disorders and Comorbidities in Children, Adolescents and Adults*. American Psychiatric Press.

Cooper, P. and Ideus, K. (eds) (1997) *Attention Deficit Hyperactivity Disorder: Educational, Medical and Cultural Issues*. Maidstone: Association of Workers for Children with Emotional and Behavioural Difficulties.

MTA Cooperative Group (2004) 'National Institute of Mental Health Multimodal Treatment Study of AD/HD. Follow-up: 24-month outcomes of treatment strategies for AD/HD'. *Pediatrics*, **113**, 754–61.

Nadeau, K.G. (1995) *A Comprehensive Guide to Attention Deficit Disorder in Adults – Research Diagnosis, Treatment*. Brunner/Mazel.

Nadeau, K.G., Littman, E. and Quinn, P. (1999) *Understanding Girls with AD/HD*. Advantage Books.

Pliszka, S.R., Carlson, C.L. and Swanson, J.M. (1999) *AD/HD with Comorbid Disorders*. Guilford Press.

Reiff, M., Tippins, S. (2004) 'AD/HD: A Complete and Authoritative Guide'. *American Academy of Pediatrics*.

Schachar, R. and Tannock, R. (2002) 'Syndromes of hyperactivity and attention deficit', in Rutter, M. and Taylor, E. (eds) *Child and Adolescent Psychiatry* (4th edn). Blackwell Science, pp. 399–418.

Weiss, L. (1997) *Attention Deficit Disorder in Adults*. Taylor Trade Publishing.

Learning difficulties

Beitchman, J.H., Young, A.R. (1997) 'Learning disorders with special emphasis on reading disorders: a review of the past 10 years'. *Journal of the American Academy of Child and Adolescent Psychiatry*, **36**, 1020–32.

Cantwell, D. and Baker, L. (1991) 'Association between Attention Deficit/Hyperactivity Disorder and learning disorders'. *Journal of Learning Disabilities*, **24**(2), 88–95.

Hechtman, L., Abikoff, H., Klein, R., Weiss, G. *et al.* (2004) 'Academic achievement and emotional status of children with AD/HD treated with long term methylphenidate and multimodal psychosocial treatment'. *Journal of the American Academy of Child and Adolescent Psychiatry*, **43**(7), 812–19.

Johnson, M. and Peer, L. (2004) *The Dyslexia Handbook 2004*. British Dyslexia Association.

Bipolar disorder

Findling, R., Kowatch, R. and Post, R. (2003) *Pediatric Bipolar Disorder – A Handbook for Clinicians*. Martin Dunitz.

Geller, B. and Luby, J. (1997) 'Child and adolescent bipolar disorder: a review of the past 10 years'. *Journal of the American Academy of Child and Adolescent Psychiatry*, **36**, 1168–76.

Lynn, G.T. (2000) *Survival Strategies for Parenting Children with Bipolar Disorder*. Jessica Kingsley Publications.

Speech and language

Beitchman, J.H., Wilson, B., Brownlie, E.B., Walters, H. *et al.* (1996) 'Long term consistency in speech/language profiles 1 & 2'. *Journal of American Academy of Child and Adolescent Psychiatry*, **35**, 804–14, 815–25.

Heyer, J.L. (1995) 'The responsibilities of speech/language pathologists towards children with AD/HD'. *Seminars in Speech and Language*, **16**(4), 275–88.

Purves, K.L. and Tannock, R. (1997) 'Language disabilities in children with ADHD, reading disabilities and normal controls'. *Journal of Abnormal Child Psychology*, **25**, 133–44.

Co-ordination

Gilberg, C. (2003) 'Deficits in attention, motor control and perception: a brief review'. *Archives of Diseases in Childhood*, **88**(10), 904–10.

Substance abuse

Biederman, J. (2003) 'Pharmacotherapy for AD/HD reduces the risk of substance abuse'. *Journal of Clinical Psychiatry*, **64**, 3–8.

Faraone, S., Mick, E., Wozniak, J. *et al.* (1997) 'Is AD/HD a risk factor for psychoactive substance abuse disorders?' *Journal of the American Academy of Child and Adolescent Psychiatry*, **6**, 21–9.

Rey, J. M., Martin, A. and Crabman, P. (2004) 'Cannabis and juvenile psychiatric disorder: the past 10 years'. *Journal of the American Academy of Child and Adolescent Psychiatry*, **43**(10), 1194–1205.

Tourette Syndrome

Chowdhury, U. (2004) *Tics and Tourette Syndrome*. Jessica Kingsley Publications.

Chowdhury, U. and Heyman, I. (2004) 'Tourette Syndrome'. *BMJ*, **329**, 1356–7.

Commins, D.E. (1996) *The Search for the Tourette's Syndrome and Human Behaviour Genes*. Duarte, CA: Hope Press.

Asperger's Syndrome

Attwood, T. (1998) *Asperger's Syndrome: A Guide for Parents and Professionals*. Jessica Kingsley Publications.

Cohen, C. (2000) *Raise Your Child's Social IQ*. Advantage Books.

Stoddart, K.P. (2005) *Children, Youth and Adults with Asperger Syndrome – Integrating Multiple Perspectives*. Jessica Kingsley Publications.

Auditory processing

Cleveland, S. (1997) 'Central auditory processing disorder: When is evaluation referral indicated?' *ADHD Report*, **5**(5), 9–12.

http://www.apduk.org

http://www.ncapd.org

Self-esteem

Brooks, R. and Goldstein, G. (2001) *Raising Resilient Children*. New York: Contemporary Books.

Cohen, C. (2000) *Raise your Child's Social IQ*. Advantage Books.

Teenagers

Barkley, R.A., Murphy, K.R. and Kwasnik, D. (1996) 'Motor vehicle driving competences and risk in teens and young adults with AD/HD'. *Paediatrics*, **98**, 1089–95.

Dendy, C.Z. (1995) *Teenagers with ADD – A Parents' Guide*. Woodbine House.

Dendy, C.Z. (2000) *Teaching Teens with ADD and AD/HD*. Woodbine House.

General management

American Academy of Child and Adolescent Psychiatry (2002) 'Practice parameter for the use of stimulant medications in the treatment of children, adolescents and adults'. *Journal of the American Academy of Child and Adolescent Psychiatry*, **41**(suppl. 2), 26–49.

American Academy of Pediatrics (2001) 'Clinical practice guideline: treatment of the school-aged child with attention-deficit/hyperactivity disorder'. *Pediatrics*, **108**, 1033–44.

Barkley, R.A. (2002) 'Psychosocial treatments for AD/HD in children'. *Journal of Clinical Psychiatry*, **63**(12), 36–43.

Brasswell, L. and Bloomquist, M.L. (1991) *Cognitive/Behavioural Therapy with ADHD Children*. Guilford Press.

Fallone, G.P. (1998) 'Parent training and AD/HD'. *The ADHD Report*, **6**(2), 9–12.

Gordon, M. (1992) *My Brother's a World Class Pain – A Sibling's Guide to ADHD*. New York: DeWitt.

Jadad, A.R. *et al.* (1999) 'The treatment of AD/HD – an annotated bibliography and critical appraisal of published systematic review and meta-analysis'. *Canadian Journal of Psychiatry*, **44**, 1025–35.

Kewley, G. (1995) 'Medical aspects of the assessment and treatment of children with ADD', in Cooper, P. and Ideus, K. (eds) *Association of Workers for Children with Emotional and Behavioural Difficulties*, pp. 31–7.

Kutcher, S. (2004) 'International consensus statement on AD/HD and disruptive behaviour disorders'. *European Neuropsychopharmacology*, **14**, 11–18.

Lord, J. and Paisley, S. (2000) *The Clinical Effectiveness and Cost-effectiveness of Methylphenidate for Hyperactivity in Children*. London: National Institute for Clinical Excellence (www.nice.org.uk).

MTA Cooperative Group (1999) 'A 14-month randomised clinical trial of treatment strategies for attention-deficit/hyperactivity disorder: multimodal treatment study of children with AD/HD'. *Arch General Psychiatry*, **56**, 1073–86.

National Institute for Clinical Excellence (2000) *Guidance on the Use of Methylphenidate for Attention Deficit/Hyperactivity Disorder (AD/HD) in Childhood*. Technology Appraisal Guideline no. 13 (www.nice.org.uk).

Scottish Intercollegiate Guidelines Network (2001) *Attention Deficit and Hyperkinetic Disorders in Children and Young People: A National Clinical Guideline*. Edinburgh: SIGN.

Sonuga-Bark, E., Daley, D. and Thompson, M. (2001) 'Parent based therapies for AD/HD'. *Journal of the American Academy of Child and Adolescent Psychiatry*, **41**, 696–702.

Taylor, E. *et al.* (2004) 'Clinical guidelines for hyperkinetic disorder – first upgrade'. *European Child Adolescent Psychiatry*, **13** (suppl.1), 17 : 30.

Webster-Stratton, C. (1998) 'Preventing conduct problems in headstart children: strengthening parent competencies'. *Journal of Consulting and Clinical Psychology*, **66**, 715–30.

Wilens, T.E. (2004) *Straight Talk About Psychiatric Medications for Kids*. Guilford Press.

Education

Cooper, P. and Ideus, K. (1996) *Attention Deficit Hyperactivity Disorder: A Practical Guide for Teachers*. David Fulton Publishers.

Cowne, E. (2003) *The SENCO Handbook* (4th edn). David Fulton Publishers.

Dendy, C.A.Z. (2000) *Teaching Teens with ADD and AD/HD*. Woodbine House.

DfES (2004) *Removing Barriers to Achievement: The Government's Strategy for SEN*. DfES Publications (dfes@prolog.uk.com).

DuPaul, G.J. and Stoner, G. (2003) *AD/HD in Schools: Assessment and Intervention Strategies*. Guilford Press.

Gabbitas Educational Consultants (2000) *The Gabbitas Guide to Schools for Special Needs*. Kogan Page.

Hechtman, L., Abikoff, H., Klein, R., Weiss, G. *et al.* (2004) 'Academic achievement and emotional status of children with AD/HD treated with long term methylphenidate and multimodal psychosocial treatment'. *Journal of the American Academy of Child and Adolescent Psychiatry*, **43**(7), 812–19.

Long-term outlook

Barkley, R.A. (2002) 'Major life activity and outcomes associated with attention-deficit/ hyperactivity disorder'. *Journal of Clinical Psychiatry*, **63**, 10–15.

Brassett-Grundy, A. and Butler, N. (2004) *Prevalence and Adult Outcomes of AD/HD – evidence from a 30-year perspective longitudinal study*. Bedford Group for Lifecourse and Statistical Studies (www.ioe.ac.uk/bedfordgroup).

Gilberg, C., Melander, H., Van Knorring, A.L., Janols, L. *et al.* (1997) 'Long term stimulant treatment of children with attention deficit hyperactivity disorder symptoms'. *Arch General Psychiatry*, **54**, 857–64.

Mannuzza, S., Klein, R.G., Bressler, A., Maloy, P. and Hynes, M.E. (1997) 'Educational and occupational outcome of hyperactive boys grown up'. *Journal of the American Academy of Child and Adolescent Psychiatry*, **36**, 1222–7.

Moffitt, T.E., Caspi, A., Dickson, N., Silva, P. and Stanton, W. (1996) 'Childhood-onset versus adolescent-onset antisocial conduct in males: natural history from age 3 to 18'. *Development and Psychopathology*, **8**, 399–424.

Weiss, G. and Heckman, L.T. (1993) *Hyperactive Children Grown Up*. Guilford Press.

Causes of AD/HD

Barkley, R.A. (1997) *ADHD and the Nature of Self-Control*. Guilford Press.

Levy, F., Hay, D.A., McStephen, M., Wood, C. and Wildman, I. (1997) 'Attention deficit hyperactivity disorder: a category or a continuum? Genetic analysis of a large scale twin study'. *Journal of the American Academy of Child and Adolescent Psychiatry*, **36**, 737–44.

Tannock, R. (1998) 'ADHD: advances in cognitive, neurobiological and genetic research'. *Journal of Child Psychology and Psychiatry*, **39**(1), 65–99.

Professionals and services for AD/HD

Australian National Health and Medical Research Council (1996) *Report of Working Party on ADHD*. Canberra: Australian Government Publishing Service.

British Psychological Society (1996) *ADHD: A Psychological Response to an Evolving Concept*.

Coghill, D. (2004) 'Use of stimulants for attention deficit hyperactivity disorder'. *British Medical Journal*, **329**, 907–8.

Cooper, P., Kewley, G., Prior, P., Reason, R. and Visser, J. (1997) 'The myth of attention deficit hyperactivity disorder: notes towards a constructive perspective on AD/HD' (collection of papers). *British Psychological Society Editorial Section Review*, **21**(1), 3–27.

Dulcan, M.K. and Benson, R.S. (1997) 'Practice parameters for the assessment and treatment of children, adolescents and adults with AD/HD'. *Journal of the American Academy of Child and Adolescent Psychiatry*, **36**, 1311–17.

Kewley, G. (1998) Personal Paper: 'ADHD is underdiagnosed and undertreated in Britain'. *British Medical Journal*, **316**, 1594–5.

Prior, P. (1997) 'ADHD/Hyperkinetic Disorder: How should educational psychologists and other practitioners respond to the emerging phenomenon of school children diagnosed as having ADHD?' *Emotional and Behavioural Difficulties*, **2**, 15–27.

Reason, R. and Sharp, S. (eds) (1997) 'ADHD: perspectives from educational psychology'. *Ed Child Psychology*, **14**(1).

Vivian, L. (1994) 'The changing pupil population of schools with emotional and behavioural difficulties'. *Therapeutic Care and Education*, **3**(3), 218–31.

Books for younger children

Blume, J. (1985) *The Pain and the Great One*. Heinemann.

Galvin, M. (1988) *Otto Learns about His Medicine*. New York: Magination Press.

Gordon, M. (1991) *Jumpin' Johnny Get Back to Work!* New York: GSI Publications.

Gordon, M. (1992) *My Brother's a World Class Pain*. New York: GSI Publications.

Moss, D. (1989) *Shelley, the Hyperactive Turtle*. Rockville: Woodbine House.

Neuville, M. (1991) *Sometimes I Get Scribbly*. La Crosse, WI: Crystal Press.

Parker, R.N. (1992) *Slam Dunk: A Young Boy's Struggle with ADD*. Florida: Impact Publications.

Quinn, P. and Stern, J. (1991) *Putting On the Brakes*. New York: Magination Press.

Quinn, P. and Stern, J. (1993) *The Putting On the Brake Activity Book for Young People with ADHD*. New York: Magination Press.

Appendix 2: Research evidence for causes of AD/HD

Research evidence for AD/HD comes from tests of brain dysfunction, family studies, genetic studies and neurophysiological theories.

Brain structure and function

There are three basic levels of brain function:

- The reticular activating system is the oldest, most primitive part of the brain. This acts as a filtering system and monitors and controls the input from the environment. Thus, only information that appears relevant and interesting is passed on to other areas of the brain. It monitors the level of cortical stimulation and alertness, and is involved in thinking, emotional and automatic function. It can inhibit or stimulate information from all senses, from the cortex, the muscles and the sense organs.

- The limbic system modulates emotions, memory and some aspects of concentration. It helps control motivation, feelings of love, hate, anger, and sadness. It controls wild and savage emotions as well as gentle and loving ones. It is therefore a crucial and very complex area, and a great many different emotional reactions are involved. Close to this is the basal ganglia where movement and sensory function are modulated. Motor functions are affected by the basal ganglia. Problems in this area may be implicated in Tourette's Syndrome and Obsessive Compulsive Disorder, as well as Parkinson's Disease.

- The outer layer, the cerebral cortex, stores, integrates and initiates complex language, cognitive thought processes, motor activities and the emotions and feelings that might come through from the limbic system. In AD/HD, the evidence suggests that this 'braking' system is not always working properly, and thus emotions that develop in the other systems may develop without the inhibition. There is some evidence that these areas are different in boys and girls. In particular, the frontal cortex is the area of executive function of response inhibition and short-term memory and integrates the other areas, which are closely interlinked.

Defects in a wide range of sites at different levels of the brain could result in problems in inattention, hyperactivity and impulsiveness. Depending on which site has defects, different additional problems – such as emotional difficulties, problems in filtering information, problems in motor control – may also be present. This may, in part, explain why medications may work in some children, but not in others, and why children with AD/HD have such a wide range of presentations. It is interesting that throughout these areas, dopamine is a very important neurotransmitter.

Tests of brain dysfunction

A number of scanning techniques have been used to look at the structure and function of the brain. These include:

■ Quantitative EEG studies: computerised EEG or electrical brainwave activity studies look at brain function, and have shown an abnormality in 85–90 per cent of cases in children and adolescents with AD/HD. This involves the normal background brainwave activity which is present in everyone. The pattern of waves is different in most children with AD/HD compared to a normal population. The particular abnormalities involve the frontal parts of the brain. The abnormal patterns frequently change to a more normal pattern with the appropriate medications. Databases are now being developed to estimate which medication is likely to be effective in individual children. These techniques are non-invasive and probably have the potential to be most effective in clinical practice.

■ Event-related potential: this is the EEG response to an auditory or visual stimulus. Most studies in children with AD/HD show that the P300 (P3b) wave is less well formed. This is thought to be involved in active working memory. Abnormal brainstem auditory evoked potentials suggest that early processing of auditory information may also be impaired in children with AD/HD.

■ Functional Magnetic Resonance scans (fMRI): functional MRI scans study brain structure and function. Recent studies have also shown that some parts of the brain that are implicated in AD/HD are not as well developed in children with AD/HD as in other children. Decreased brain activation has been shown in some areas of the right hemisphere with increased activation in sub-cortical areas.

■ Structural MRI and CT scans: whilst allowing for changes with age and between the sexes, there are persistent findings of localised abnormalities in the pre-frontal cortex, basal ganglia and corpus callosum in children with AD/HD. These findings are in keeping with theoretical models of abnormal brain function in AD/HD.

■ Positron Emission Tomography scans (PET): these scans use functional/dynamic techniques to study brain metabolism and regional changes in brain activity. For example, scans of adults with AD/HD have shown widespread, bilateral decrease in glucose metabolism, especially in the pre-motor cortex and superior frontal cortices. A subsequent study in adolescents showed minimal and non-significant findings. Females tend to show more abnormalities than males. At present the effects of stimulant medication on cerebral glucose metabolism have not been fully assessed.

■ Brain chemistry studies: the brain is composed of millions of neurones, or nerve cells, each with branches known as dendrites. The cells are joined by synapses or 'junction boxes' and the messages go from one cell to another via neurotransmitters – chemicals that allow the message to get across the synapse. The areas of the brain involved in AD/HD are normally particularly rich in chemicals known as dopamine and norepinephrine. Studies in rats show that when the brain areas containing dopamine are destroyed the rats become very hyperactive and this could be improved with stimulant medication.

Family studies

Many family studies have shown a higher than normal prevalence of AD/HD and other psychopathology, including depressive anxiety disorders, substance abuse, oppositional and conduct disorders, in families and first-degree relatives of children with AD/HD. Approximately 40 per cent of the parents of these children have, or have had, symptoms of AD/HD themselves, and about 30 per cent of non-twin brothers and sisters may also have AD/HD.

- Other factors, such as difficult birth, environmental problems or family stress are important, but much less so, although prematurity confers a greatly increased risk of AD/HD, irrespective of family history.

- Twin studies show an exceptionally high inheritance, compared with other behavioural disorders. These studies also show that AD/HD symptoms are a continuum so that, like height, weight and blood pressure, AD/HD is present when these symptoms are far enough away from normal. This increased chance of the second twin having AD/HD if the first one already has it, is much greater than would be expected if only non-hereditary factors were involved.

Such studies show that at least 80 per cent of the causation of AD/HD is due to genetics and suggest a strong genetic basis for AD/HD. These studies have also shown the environment to have very little effect on the core AD/HD symptoms.

- Adoption studies: the incidence of AD/HD in adopted children is significantly higher than in other children, even allowing for environmental difficulties or earlier abuse. When adoption has occurred at birth or shortly thereafter, the presence of later AD/HD symptoms cannot be explained solely by environmental problems or attachment disorders. Studies have shown higher rates of hyperactivity in biological parents of children with AD/HD. If one of the biological parents had a history of criminal convictions or delinquency, the adopted children were also more likely to have AD/HD. A very significant number of children born to young parents with AD/HD are placed in care.

The increased incidence of AD/HD in adopted children may be partly because:

- young parents with AD/HD are simply less likely to be able to cope with parenthood;

- young women may have become pregnant impulsively: studies show that impulsivity is involved in a high percentage of teenage pregnancies;

- their fathers are more likely to be conduct-disordered adolescent males.

Long-term studies show that, compared with a non-AD/HD population, adolescents and adults with AD/HD have many more pregnancies, are less likely to use birth control methods and are more likely to have contracted a sexually transmitted disease.

Genetic studies

A number of genes seem to be involved in affecting human behaviour, especially those linked to the production of dopamine. The mode of inheritance of AD/HD is uncertain, most researchers favouring the involvement of a number of genes, though some studies do suggest that a single major gene may be involved. The implication of genes coding for the dopamine system fits well with imaging studies which demonstrate that the areas of the brain linked to AD/HD are generally dopamine-rich.

The D4 Dopamine Receptor Gene (DRD4), in its seven-repeat gene form, has been shown by several investigations to be present more often in people with AD/HD and Novelty-Seeking Personality than in others. Some researchers have proposed abnormalities in the Dopamine Transporter Gene (DAT I) and in Dopamine Type 2 Gene. Other gene deficits are increasingly being reported, and no doubt the next few years will see an explosion of knowledge.

Some genes are found in increased incidence not only in AD/HD but also in Tourette's Syndrome, people with substance abuse problems, chronic early onset alcoholism, compulsive gamblers and those with other problems related to impulse control and inhibition.

Genetic studies increasingly suggest that AD/HD is based on genetic abnormalities within the dopamine system. However, much more research is needed to establish the number of genes involved, how they interact with the environment, how heritable they are and whether or not they have additive effects.

Neuropsychological theories

Some researchers have considered that attention and cognitive problems form the basis of AD/HD and that hyperactivity/impulsiveness is but one of a number of possible sub-clusters which include problems in starting and organising work, in sustained attention, in sustaining energy and effort, in moodiness and sensitivity to criticism and in memory recall.

However, for types of AD/HD other than the predominantly inattentive group, the theory proposed by Professor R. Barkley, Professor of Psychology and Psychiatry at the University of Massachusetts, explains many of the features previously inexplicable in children with AD/HD, and seems to best fit the clinical situation. Central to the theory is the fact that by not delaying their immediate response to an event, people with AD/HD have subsequent difficulties in executive function. AD/HD therefore is best seen as a condition of behavioural disinhibition that creates problems with the executive abilities.

- First executive function: working memory. By delaying the event and not responding with the first impulsive reaction, that event is momentarily kept in mind and thought about transiently to devise the most satisfactory response. Thinking about the response may well change the way a person eventually acts. In AD/HD, where there is difficulty in inhibiting a response, the events are not kept in short-term memory, and a less satisfactory outcome is more likely.

  This difficulty in short-term memory and keeping events in mind leads to difficulties in:
  - awareness of time, the past and the future. In speech they make fewer comments about the past and the future.
  - learning from mistakes
  - waiting, as time tends to pass more slowly
  - directing their behaviour towards the future, as they tend to live in the moment
  - disorganisation
  - time management

- Second executive function: controlling feelings and emotions. This is the ability to delay one's emotional response to a situation, to have the chance to analyse it and decide on the most appropriate, usually less emotive, response, and be more objective. It also enables one to inhibit one's own emotions to achieve longer-term goals.

Difficulty in controlling feelings and emotions leads to difficulties in:
- achieving longer-term goals, without reacting to the more immediate day-to-day difficulties
- motivation, drive and the ability to keep going with a task if there are not frequent short-term rewards
- emotional impulsivity, tending to show their often immature emotions very readily.

■ Third executive function: self-directed speech. The ability to inhibit seems to be related to the ability to internalise language, to think through for oneself the possible options and then use this as a way of helping control one's behaviour. People with AD/HD do not use self-directed speech as well, or as effectively, as those without. By not inhibiting their initial reaction, they are less reflective.

Difficulty in controlling self-directed speech leads to difficulties in:
- rule-governed behaviour
- free will
- considering all possible solutions to a problem
- sequencing and verbal fluency
- communication
- producing disjointed ideas and behaviour patterns
- writing
- organisation of ideas and coherency.

Thus, people with AD/HD have serious problems in self-control and self-regulation. This goes against the widespread assumption that all individuals have equal degrees of self-control, which does not allow much margin for people with AD/HD, who tend to be chaotic, not to see the problems ahead, and who need a great deal of structure and organisation in their lives.

Appendix 3: Diagnostic criteria

DSM-IV diagnostic criteria for Attention Deficit/ Hyperactivity Disorder*

A. Either 1. or 2.:

1. Six (or more) of the following symptoms of inattention have persisted for at least six months to a degree that is maladaptive and inconsistent with developmental level:

Inattention

(a) often fails to give close attention to details or makes careless mistakes in schoolwork, work or other activities

(b) often has difficulty sustaining attention in tasks or play activities

(c) often does not seem to listen when spoken to directly

(d) often does not follow through on instructions and fails to finish schoolwork, chores or duties in the workplace (not due to oppositional behaviour or failure to understand instructions)

(e) often has difficulty organising tasks and activities

(f) often avoids, dislikes or is reluctant to engage in tasks that require sustained mental effort (such as schoolwork or homework)

(g) often loses things necessary for tasks or activities (e.g. toys, school assignments, pencils, books, tools)

(h) often is easily distracted by extraneous stimuli

(i) often is forgetful in daily activities

2. Six (or more) of the following symptoms of hyperactivity-impulsivity have persisted for at least six months to a degree that is maladaptive and inconsistent with developmental level:

Hyperactivity

(a) often fidgets with hands or feet or squirms in seat

(b) often leaves seat in classroom or in other situations in which remaining seated is expected

(c) often runs about or climbs excessively in situations in which it is inappropriate (in adolescents or adults, may be limited to subjective feelings of restlessness)

(d) often has difficulty playing or engaging in leisure activities quietly

(e) often is 'on the go' or acts as if 'driven by a motor'

(f) often talks excessively

Impulsivity

(g) often blurts out answers before questions have been completed

(h) often has difficulty awaiting turn

(i) often interrupts or intrudes on others (e.g. butts into conversations or games)

B. Some hyperactive-impulsive or inattentive symptoms that caused impairment were present before age 7.

C. Some impairment from the symptoms is present in two or more settings (e.g. at school [or work] and at home).

D. There must be clear evidence of clinically significant impairment in social, academic or occupational functioning.

E. The symptoms do not occur exclusively during the course of a Pervasive Developmental Disorder, Schizophrenia or other Psychotic Disorder and are not better accounted for by another mental disorder (e.g. Mood Disorder, Anxiety Disorder, Dissociative Disorder, Personality Disorder).

Code based on type:

314.01 Attention Deficit/Hyperactivity Disorder, Combined Type: if both Criteria Al and A2 are met for the past six months.

314.00 Attention Deficit/Hyperactivity Disorder, Predominantly Inattentive Type: if Criterion Al is met but Criterion A2 is not met for the past six months.

314.01 Attention Deficit/Hyperactivity Disorder, Predominantly Hyperactive-Impulsive Type: if Criterion A2 is met but Criterion Al is not met for the past six months.

Coding note: For individuals (especially adolescents and adults) who currently have symptoms that no longer meet full criteria, 'In Partial Remission' should be specified.

DSM-IV diagnostic criteria for 313.80 Oppositional Defiant Disorder*

A. A pattern of negativistic, hostile and defiant behaviour lasting at least six months, during which four (or more) of the following are present:

(a) often loses temper

(b) often argues with adults

(c) often actively defies or refuses to comply with adults' requests or rules

(d) often deliberately annoys people

(e) often blames others for his or her mistakes or behaviour

(f) often is touchy or easily annoyed by others

(g) often is angry and resentful

(h) often is spiteful or vindictive

Note: Consider a criterion only if the behaviour occurs more frequently than is typically observed in individuals of comparable age and developmental level.

B. The disturbance in behaviour causes clinically significant impairment in social, academic or occupational functioning.

C. The behaviours do not occur exclusively during the course of a Psychotic or Mood Disorder.

D. Criteria are not met for Conduct Disorder and, if the individual is age 18 or older, criteria are not met for Antisocial Personality Disorder.

DSM-IV diagnostic criteria for 312.8 Conduct Disorder*

A. A repetitive and persistent pattern of behaviour in which the basic rights of others or major age-appropriate societal norms or rules are violated, as manifested by the presence of three (or more) of the following criteria in the past 12 months, with at least one criterion present in the past six months:

Aggression to people and animals

(a) often bullies, threatens or intimidates others

(b) often initiates physical fights

(c) has used a weapon that can cause serious physical harm to others (e.g. a bat, brick, broken bottle, knife, gun)

(d) has been physically cruel to people

(e) has been physically cruel to animals

(f) has stolen while confronting a victim (e.g. mugging, purse snatching, extortion, armed robbery)

(g) has forced someone into sexual activity

Destruction of property

(h) has deliberately engaged in fire-setting with the intention of causing serious damage

(i) has deliberately destroyed others' property (other than by fire-setting) – deceitfulness or theft

(j) has broken into someone else's house, building or car

(k) often lies to obtain goods or favours or to avoid obligations (i.e. 'cons' others)

(l) has stolen items of non-trivial value without confronting a victim and without breaking and entering (e.g. shoplifting, forgery)

Serious violations of rules

(m) often stays out at night despite parental prohibitions; beginning before age 13

(n) has run away from home overnight at least twice while living in parental or parental surrogate home (or once without returning for a lengthy period)

(o) often truants from school, beginning before age 13

B. The disturbance in behaviour causes clinically significant impairment in social, academic, or occupational functioning.

C. If the individual is age 18 or older, criteria are not met for Antisocial Personality Disorder.

Specify type based on age at onset:

Childhood-Onset Type: onset of at least one criterion characteristic of Conduct Disorder prior to age 10

Adolescent-Onset Type: absence of any criteria characteristic of Conduct Disorder prior to age 10

Specify severity:

Mild: few, if any, conduct problems in excess of those required to make the diagnosis and conduct problems cause only minor harm to others.

Moderate: number of conduct problems and effect on others intermediate between 'mild' and 'severe'

Severe: many conduct problems in excess of those required to make the diagnosis or conduct problems cause considerable harm to others.

DSM-IV Criteria for Tourette's Disorder*

A. Both multiple motor and one or more vocal tics have been present at some time during the illness, although not necessarily concurrently. (A tic is a sudden, rapid, recurrent, non-rhythmic, stereotyped motor movement or vocalisation.)

B. The tics occur many times a day (usually in bouts) nearly every day or intermittently throughout a period of more than one year, and during this period there was never a tic-free period of more than three consecutive months.

C. The disturbance causes marked distress or significant impairment in social, occupational or other important areas of functioning.

D. The onset is before age 18.

E. The disturbance is not due to the direct physiological effects of a substance (e.g. stimulants) or a general medical condition (e.g. Huntington's disease or post-viral encephalitis).

Appendix 4: Useful addresses

Learning Assessment and Neurocare Centre
48–50 Springfield Road
Horsham
West Sussex
RH12 2PD
Tel: 01403 240002
Fax: 01403 260900
Email: info@lanc.uk.com
www.lanc.uk.com

Multidisciplinary clinic for assessment and management of children and adults with neurodevelopmental, behavioural and learning difficulties, especially AD/HD and related conditions.

ADD Information Services
The ADDISS Resource Centre
PO Box 340
Edgware
Middlesex
HA8 9HL
Tel: 020 8906 9068
Fax: 020 8959 0727
Email: info@addiss.co.uk
www.addiss.co.uk

Produces a wide range of books on AD/HD and related subjects.
Helpful information and advice and details of local support groups.

Advisory Centre for Education (ACE)
Unit 1B
Aberdeen Studios
22 Highbury Grove
London N5 2DQ
Tel: 020 7354 8321

National Autistic Association
393 City Road
London EC1V 1NG
Tel: 020 7833 2299

OAASIS
Brock House
Grigg Lane
Brockenhurst
Hants
SO42 7RE

British Dyslexia Association
98 London Road
Reading
RG1 5AU
Tel: 0118 966 8271

The Dyspraxia Trust
PO Box 30
Hitchin
Herts
SG5 1UU
Tel: 01462 454986

Independent Panel for Special Educational Advice (IPSEA)
22 Warren Hill Road
Woodbridge
Suffolk
IP12 4DU
Tel: 01394 382814

Tourette Syndrome (UK) Association
PO Box 26149
Dunfermline
KY12 7YU
Tel: 0845 458 1252

National Resource Centre on AD/HD – US CHADD
8181 Professional Place
Suite 150
Landover
Maryland 20785
www.help4adhd.org; www.chadd.org

Support groups

A full list of support groups in local areas is available from ADD Information Services or on the ADD Internet Service.

Index

DATE DUE
